$25.45

DISCARDED

REGAINING
THE DREAM

REGAINING THE DREAM

How to Renew the Promise of Homeownership for America's Working Families

ROBERTO G. QUERCIA

ALLISON FREEMAN

JANNEKE RATCLIFFE

BROOKINGS INSTITUTION PRESS
Washington, D.C.

Library of Congress Cataloging-in-Publication data
Quercia, Roberto G.
Regaining the dream : how to renew the promise of homeownership for
America's working families / Roberto G. Quercia, Allison Freeman, Janneke
Ratcliffe.
    p.   cm.
Includes bibliographical references and index.
Summary: "Backed by extensive study of mortgage loans made to low-income
Americans over a ten-year period, argues that in the wake of the financial crisis
of 2008-09, lenders need not shy away from the low-income as risks but insti-
tute equitable and sustainable homeownership policies that include correctly
structured loans"—Provided by publisher.
  ISBN 978-0-8157-2172-7 (pbk. : alk. paper)
  1. Housing—United States--Finance. 2. Working class—Housing—United
States. 3. Mortgage loans—United States. 4. Homeownership—United States.
I. Freeman, Allison. II. Ratcliffe, Janneke. III. Title.
  HD7293.Z9Q47 2011
  332.7'20973—dc23   2011022122

9 8 7 6 5 4 3 2 1

Printed on acid-free paper

Typeset in Sabon

Composition by Oakland Street Publishing
Arlington, Virginia

Printed by R. R. Donnelley
Harrisonburg, Virginia

Contents

Foreword

This book describes an astonishing journey that began in 1998. That was the year in which the Ford Foundation, Fannie Mae, and a small group of banks subscribed to the vision of an audacious non-profit organization in North Carolina that set out to make home-ownership possible for low-income renters, to reduce the racial wealth gap, and to make a fair profit for primary lenders, secondary market institutions, and itself in the process. The organization—Self-Help Ventures Fund—convinced each of the parties to join it in a demonstration to enable at least 40,000 low-income and minority households to become homeowners.

At the Ford Foundation, we were excited about the partnership. We saw an historic opportunity to show how to eliminate systemic barriers to homeownership for low-income and minority families if the secondary market institutions would only begin to purchase the sound, customized community reinvestment mortgages being underwritten by many of the nation's banks. Because so little evidence was available regarding the performance of affordable mortgages for low-income and minority households and the financial and social impacts of home-ownership on these families, we put in place a long-term research project to track the performance of the mortgages and the effects of owning a home on the families.

Little did we realize how other powerful forces were gathering at the same time to undermine the very work on which we were embarking. Within a decade, unsafe, mispriced, and underregulated lending would decimate household wealth, particularly among minority families, and leave the U.S. housing finance system a wreck. We also did not recognize at that time the extraordinary timeliness and relevance the evidence gleaned from the research would have as the country now sets out to chart a new way forward for the housing finance system and the future of homeownership. *Regaining the Dream* offers lessons to inform both of these critical issues. And it reaffirms the Ford Foundation's belief that homeownership for low-income and minority households can be encouraged responsibly and sustainably—that it is critical to assist these households to build assets and to close the pernicious and persistent racial wealth gap in this country.

One of the goals of the Ford Foundation is to reduce poverty and injustice. The foundation believes that helping low-income people acquire, control, and maintain financial assets is crucial to achieving this goal because assets provide a cushion against unexpected expenses or crises, helping households achieve an important measure of stability. Assets also serve as a platform for upward mobility, enabling households to invest in their future in a variety of ways, such as pursuing an education or starting a business.

Recognition of the importance of assets to economic mobility led the foundation to promote homeownership among low-income and minority households because historically equity in a home has been the single largest financial asset for most Americans. Home equity remains an important component of family balance sheets, representing nearly half of total family assets among all but the very highest earners.[1] The decision to promote homeownership was reinforced by the substantial disparities in homeownership that existed among income and racial groups. In the early 1990s the homeownership rate for families in the upper income quintile was more than twice that of the lowest.[2] The disparity in homeownership among racial groups was equally striking: seven in ten white families owned their home, compared to four in ten African American and Hispanic American families.[3] Because homes are the single largest asset for most families, the disparities in home-ownership were reflected in the sizable wealth gaps between income and racial groups. At the start of the 1990s, low-income households had less than 5 percent of the net worth of the typical U.S household. Similarly, minority households had less than a tenth of that of white households. Thus we hoped that increasing homeownership rates among low-income and minority households would allow them to build financial assets, achieve economic mobility, and begin to close the wealth gap.

The opportunity to address these disparities presented itself in 1998, when Self-Help Ventures Fund, the home and business lending arm of a small North Carolina community development financial institution, proposed an extraordinarily large idea. It asked the foundation for a $50 million grant to create a national secondary market for community reinvestment home loans.

Four years earlier—with only $55 million in total assets at the time—Self-Help had acquired a $20 million affordable home loan portfolio from a North Carolina bank. It had leveraged an impressive record of loan repayment with that portfolio to convince Fannie Mae that its model for mortgage lending done right could expand home-ownership to creditworthy low-income and minority working families. Self-Help now turned to us. Our grant to Self-Help launched what was then the largest homeownership demonstration in the United States, the Community Advantage Program, or CAP. The pioneering project guaranteed the sale of $2 billion worth of nonconforming mortgages to Fannie Mae, thereby expanding homeownership opportunities for low-income and minority families.

Once CAP was up and running, we launched the long-term research study to document the experience of the low-income borrowers who received CAP loans. We wanted to understand, in as comprehensive and detailed a way as possible, whether and how low-income and minority families benefited from homeownership. These results, we hoped, would allay concerns that owning a home exposed low-income people to excessive stress and risk. Equally important, we hoped that rigorous analysis of the performance of the mortgages over time would reveal that the actual risk associated with these mortgages was much less than the lending industry perceived. The ultimate goal of the demonstration, beyond assisting 40,000 low-income households to become homeowners, was to change the way the financial industry approached the provision of mortgage financing for low-income and minority households.

Since 1999 our research partner in this work, the University of North Carolina at Chapel Hill's Center for Community Capital, has closely tracked the performance of each of the 46,000 affordable home loans involved in the demonstration. Center researchers also have interviewed more than 2,000 of the homeowners each year for the past six years to learn what the opportunity to buy a home with a CAP mortgage has meant for their household.

The project and the research were timely. Starting before the financial crisis and extending through to today, the researchers have been able to observe and capture in great detail the experience of these homeowners through the best and worst of times. Despite the recent upheaval in U.S. mortgage markets, thousands of low-income and minority borrowers have navigated an affordable way into sustained homeownership. From a financial perspective, the results are impressive. Even with the substantial price declines during the Great Recession, the value of homes owned by CAP borrowers increased by a median annualized rate of 2.5 percent from loan origination through the second quarter of 2009. This translates to an annualized return on equity of 36 percent. In absolute terms, CAP families experienced a median equity increase of $23,000. While this may not seem extraordinary, remember that most purchases involved very small down payments from families with few other assets. Thus even in the midst of one of the worst housing market declines in U.S. history, CAP borrowers still managed to build wealth through homeownership.

Significantly, CAP families have proven to be good credit risks. Most of the households have never missed a payment. Yes, some households experienced repayment problems, but their delinquency rate is only slightly above the serious delinquency rate for prime fixed-rate loans. It is substantially below serious delinquency rates for prime adjustable-rate loans, about one-third that of subprime fixed-rate loans, and one-fifth that of subprime adjustable-rate loans as of this writing.

The CAP borrowers' success is explained by two key factors: sound products and an effective lending process. Borrowers were provided mortgages with reasonable down payments, other financial assistance, and good preparation for homeownership from knowledgeable housing counselors. Most important, the lending process did not end at closing. Effective post-purchase support also helped to improve performance and minimize losses. Early intervention and creative servicing when delinquencies occurred helped borrowers weather financial difficulties. It is this combination of product and process that the foundation feels should form the basis of future homeownership efforts.

High default rates and concomitant loss severity for subprime loans reflect the catastrophic results of allowing bad products, improper lending processes, and inadequate regulation. The excesses in nonprime lending led to a financial crisis that affected everyone. Disproportionately affected, however, are those very communities that had long been denied equal access to housing finance; they now bear the brunt of foreclosures, ruined credit, and vacant and abandoned homes. An estimated 17 percent of Latinos and 11 percent of African Americans who were homeowners in 2006, the year before the mortgage market collapsed, are expected to lose their homes as a result of the foreclosure crisis, compared to 7 percent of non-Hispanic whites. The direct and indirect costs of foreclosure will strip an estimated $194 billion in assets from African American communities and $177 billion from Latino communities, representing the single largest loss of assets among African Americans and Latinos in modern U.S. history.[4]

Over the course of seventy years the modern U.S. housing finance system, supported and enabled by policy and regulation, developed the tools to make lending sound and widely accessible. That system enabled the Community Advantage Program to lead tens of thousands of low-income working families safely into homeownership and financial security. Unfortunately, it also spawned subprime lending, which left in its wake millions of devastated families, a U.S. housing finance system in ruins, and a global economy in shaky condition. Until now, policymakers and regulators have had little in the way of actual data to guide them in creating a system that encourages the former outcome and prevents the latter.

In *Regaining the Dream: How to Renew the Promise of Home-ownership for America's Working Families*, researchers at the UNC Center for Community Capital identify the factors that produced the very positive results for the low-income households in the CAP demonstration and argue that these factors should be the foundation for the mortgage finance system of the future. Authors Roberto G. Quercia, Allison Freeman, and Janneke Ratcliffe lay out in clear, compelling terms the reasons for the failure and meltdown of the U.S. housing finance system, what worked and what didn't work, and what can be done to lead to a sustainable housing finance system going forward.

The country needs to reexamine assumptions about low-income borrowers, homeownership, and housing policy. It needs to distinguish policies that promote homeownership as an affirmative response to intractable structural racial wealth disparities from policies that promote asset bubbles and diminished homeownership. It is useful to remember that homeownership rates topped out in the United States in 2004, well before the explosion of subprime lending and the debt-driven housing price bubble. Moving forward, the United States' public policy, regulatory climate, and mortgage systems must be designed to promote quality mortgage products and lending processes that support sustainable homeownership, particularly for low-income households. To regain the dream, it is important to identify and reinforce those elements that will increase stability and fair access to the housing finance market.

The great American middle class was built on a policy platform that began with housing finance reforms during the Great Depression. Along with access to higher education, largely a result of the GI Bill, and access to industrial jobs offering sustainable wages and good benefits, more democratic access to mortgage finance provided a unique opportunity for millions of families to enjoy intergenerational upward mobility for decades. When structural defects in housing markets and lending programs produced unacceptable racial and spatial disparities, bold policies like the Fair Housing and Community Reinvestment Acts were passed to redress them affirmatively. And yet by the end of the twentieth century it was obvious that equal access to the middle class was not a reality for large swaths of the population. Moreover, capital markets had not evolved to support adequately affirmative responses, like lending under the Community Reinvestment Act.

Today, even during the ongoing financial crisis, homeownership remains an important institution. Moreover, home equity continues to be a major part of the balance sheet of American households. Even for those households with negative equity, the majority continue to pay their mortgages on time. This shows that homeownership is more than a financial calculation for most families.

Any future housing finance system must provide a framework that ensures the flow of credit to working families who are ready to achieve and sustain homeownership. The experience of CAP borrowers during the crisis clearly demonstrates the viability of sound affordable home lending. The track record of CAP borrowers also shows that there is good business to be pursued in underserved markets. The Community Advantage Program is a model upon which to base sound and equitable lending policy.

We are very proud of the Ford Foundation's involvement in both expanding homeownership opportunities for creditworthy low-income and minority families and for helping to contribute knowledge to help restore stability to the U.S. mortgage system. It has been our great pleasure to collaborate with the innovative and committed leaders at Self-Help and with the talented and equally committed research team at the UNC Center for Community Capital in this work. We hope that the information in this book indeed helps to renew the dream of homeownership for America's working families.

Frank F. DeGiovanni
Director, Financial Assets Unit, Ford Foundation
George McCarthy
Director, Metropolitan Opportunity Unit, Ford Foundation

Acknowledgments

The Center for Community Capital at the University of North Carolina at Chapel Hill conducts research that helps policymakers, advocates, and the private sector find sustainable ways to broaden economic opportunity. Since 1999 the center has undertaken research on loans made to low- and moderate-income borrowers through a groundbreaking partnership between Self-Help (a leading community development financial institution), the Ford Foundation, and Fannie Mae. This partnership provides an unparalleled opportunity for evaluating the benefits and costs of affordable home lending. This book, a comprehensive overview of the center's research, reflects the effort and creativity of many people.

First and foremost, we acknowledge and thank Frank DeGiovanni and George McCarthy of the Ford Foundation. Their ongoing and generous support over many years has made our work possible. In addition, they have contributed substantively to our analysis by pushing us to question our assumptions, improve our data collection practices, and strengthen our analysis. Their vision has led to the creation of a rich source of data that researchers can use to answer important questions about the role of affordable homeownership in people's lives.

The center is engaged in an ongoing effort to use these data to document the effects of affordable home loans on lower income, minority, and lower wealth families in the United States. Over the last ten years, researchers at the center have produced a series of papers and policy briefs that inform a number of cutting-edge research questions.

The collective body of this work has been brought to bear on critical issues central to U.S. housing policy. We acknowledge here the many researchers responsible for this work.

In particular, we recognize Mark Lindblad, Sarah Riley, and Kim Manturuk, who have produced many rigorous studies on the economic and social impacts of homeownership. We also acknowledge several researchers who are no longer at the center but whose work is heavily referenced in this book. In particular, the work of Lei Ding, Jon Spader, and Walter Davis forms the core of chapter 3. Finally, we recognize three center collaborators: Michal Grinstein-Weiss and Clinton Key for their work on the social impacts of homeownership and Melissa Jacoby for her work on bankruptcy among low- and moderate-income borrowers. We further recognize the important contribution of the many UNC graduate students who worked for the center. The research presented here would not have been possible without their toil.

Research is not possible without data. We thank Self-Help, its lender partners, and Fannie Mae for sharing necessary data with us, loan by loan, year after year; without their doing so, we would not have a real-world context within which to answer our research questions. We also thank UNC's Survey Research Unit and RTI International for their tireless efforts in collecting household survey data. Finally, we thank the Center for Responsible Lending for its generous sharing of loan-level data.

Kathleen Kearns helped us launch the effort that culminated in this book. Her work as a developmental editor helped us clarify our thinking and map our course. Ms. Kearns also provided editorial feedback on early drafts of the book. We express our deepest gratitude for her assistance and her tireless willingness to keep us on track.

Finally, we acknowledge with gratitude Michael A. Stegman, founding director of the center. It was Dr. Stegman who designed and led the evaluation of the Community Advantage Program (CAP) for many years before leaving UNC to join the John D. and Catherine T. MacArthur Foundation as director of policy and housing. Neither the center nor this book would exist today without his groundbreaking vision and tireless work.

1 | *Foreclosing on the American Dream*

Millions of families have lost their homes since the start of the Great Recession in 2008. By mid-2010, 4.6 percent of all mortgage loans in the United States were in foreclosure, three times the rate of foreclosure at the height of the Great Depression of the 1930s.[1] Working families were left to pay for the recklessness of a market run amok, and they continue to do so through the loss of their homes, unrelenting unemployment, and stagnant wages. After the failure of more than 150 banks, the loss of over $7 trillion in homeowners' equity, and a global credit freeze, some analysts want to place the blame for these economic crises on policies that promoted homeownership rather than on the wildly irresponsible financial schemes promoted by Wall Street.[2] Is the dream of homeownership lost for America's working families?

No. It doesn't need to be. The current crisis provides an invaluable opportunity to regain the dream by expanding access to sustainable and affordable mortgages for American families. How can affordable lending be resumed without excessive risk taking? The answer lies in the experiences of low-income, low-wealth families who bought homes using traditional, well-underwritten mortgages that they could afford in the decade leading up to the crisis. We document the experiences of 46,000 of these families, who have a median income of $30,000 and most of whom put down less than 5 percent on their home purchase. Despite facing the biggest housing crisis since the Great Depression, these families have experienced low defaults, less than a quarter the level of the subprime market. Given a fair opportunity, the vast majority have successfully maintained and benefited from homeownership.

Before we explain how to regain the dream of homeownership, we step back and recall why national policy has for several decades focused on making homeownership widely accessible.

Homeownership helps families build prosperity. For many Americans, especially less affluent Americans, home equity represents the greater part of their household wealth. For generations, we Americans have viewed homeownership as the cornerstone of the American dream. We value homeownership because it signals economic advancement, promises long-term economic benefits, and represents a tangible piece of the American way of life.

Americans' homes are inviolable: they provide us with stability and security, both financial and psychological. We mark the most important events in our lives by where we lived when they occurred. Our homes also provide shelter, a reliable, long-term savings vehicle, and the chance to pass along wealth to our children. Home equity and the ability to borrow against it allow us to send our children to college, start businesses, and save for retirement. Homeownership also promotes broader economic growth as it fuels a host of construction, real estate, and financial businesses.

For all these reasons, since the 1930s U.S. housing policy has focused on enabling access to mortgage finance. The evolution of this policy is worth reviewing briefly. This history demonstrates that policy drives and shapes what markets do. More important, it shows that when policy promoting homeownership has proven to have shortcomings, it has been modified, not discarded. The effects of housing policy can be profound; thus policymaking must be an incremental process—not always the case in the past. Missteps have only emphasized the importance of getting housing policy right.

Since 1934, when the Federal Housing Administration (FHA) was established to restore confidence in a mortgage market crippled by the Great Depression, U.S. housing policy has sought to promote access to capital in ways that allowed an increasing number of families to build financial security through homeownership. One of the mortgage finance system's most important innovations is the affordable, thirty-year, fixed-rate mortgage. Widely promoted in the 1930s following the creation of FHA insurance, this long-term, low-down-payment, fully amortizing product brought down the cost of homeownership to a point where many Americans could buy into the American dream.

In a world where the adjustable-rate mortgage remains the norm, the United States is one of only three countries where long-term, fixed-rate mortgages are widely available.[3] In the United States, borrowers with fixed-rate mortgages are largely relieved of interest rate risk: interest payments do not go up when rates rise, but if rates fall borrowers can refinance to a lower rate loan. Investors in capital markets, not borrowers, bear the risk of interest rate changes. These investors buy bonds or securities backed by the value of mortgage loans in the so-called secondary mortgage market, accepting risks they can manage in proportion to the return they want.

Because of these innovations, American families can own a home with a manageable financial outlay and predictable monthly payments and, in the process, can build substantial savings. The homeownership rate in America climbed steadily following the creation of the thirty-year fixed-rate mortgage until 2004, by which point two-thirds of American households owned their own homes, compared to just 48 percent of Americans in 1930.[4]

However, the benefits of homeownership, enabled and supported by public policy, are not shared equitably. The American dream has historically been less attainable for minority households and for those with lower incomes, even though access to opportunities for economic mobility is particularly important for those with little wealth. In 2010, 74 percent of white families owned their homes, but only 45 percent of blacks and 47 percent of Latinos enjoyed the same privilege.[5] Homeownership has also been less accessible to those with lower incomes. In 2010 the homeownership rate for those with incomes in the top half was 82 percent, while for those with incomes in the bottom half it hovered at 51 percent.[6]

These disparities are in part the result of policies put in place by the federal government itself as it worked to expand mortgage lending in the 1930s. As the government began to assume much of the risk of lending in U.S. mortgage markets by backing home loans with FHA insurance, it also developed, through the Home Owner's Loan Corporation, appraisal practices and standards that undervalued dense, racially mixed, or aging neighborhoods. By definition, this rating system favored newer suburban developments to the detriment of older central cities.

As new policies favoring suburban real estate markets were created in the 1940s, so were practices determining who would have access to these markets. Now that it was undertaking much of the risk for mortgage lending, the federal government was interested in setting the lending rules. Since those informing federal policy maintained that integrated and mainly minority neighborhoods had unstable property values, the federal government advocated the preservation of mainly white neighborhoods. Toward this end, until the practice was ruled unenforceable in 1948, the FHA required that properties it insured have covenants that maintained divisions by race. Though these guidelines and practices disappeared decades ago, they shaped the form of U.S. cities and their suburbs, and their consequences remain to this day.

By the 1960s the civil rights movement put fair housing issues on the national agenda, and several legislative changes to equalize access to credit and opportunity followed. The 1968 Federal Fair Housing Act and the 1970 Equal Credit Opportunity Act prohibited certain forms of discrimination in housing and lending. In 1975 Congress enacted the Home Mortgage Disclosure Act (HMDA) so that the public might monitor access to the home mortgage market. Data gathered under HMDA confirmed an unequal distribution of credit by banks and thrifts, and in 1977 Congress passed the Community Reinvestment Act (CRA) to address these disparities.

Unlike other pieces of legislation developed during the civil rights era, the CRA did not prohibit discriminatory practices on the part of institutions but rather placed upon banks the obligation that they accommodate creditworthy households that had previously been excluded from conventional home finance. The CRA required financial institutions to meet in a sound manner the credit needs of the communities in which they were chartered. Banks responded by increasing their lending to low- and moderate-income borrowers and communities, particularly as CRA performance measurements became more quantitative in 1995. One common approach was to develop special mortgage lending programs that featured flexible guidelines.

The history of housing policy in the United States demonstrates that—for good or for ill—the government has a hand in determining how markets work to provide credit and opportunity. Following the economic shock of the Great Depression, the government acted boldly to redress a liquidity shortfall. However, the policies established during that era were skewed to help only certain categories of people. With the passage of the CRA, the government stepped in to correct the distortion in the allocation of housing credit that prior housing policies had helped to cause.

The CRA could only go so far in increasing lending to low- and moderate-income people, however, since one of the greatest determinants of which loans were issued was which loans could be sold to Fannie Mae and Freddie Mac. These two government-sponsored enterprises, created in 1938 and 1970 respectively, were designed to provide lenders with an outlet for the loans they originated. By purchasing loans from banks and thrift institutions, Fannie Mae and Freddie Mac increased liquidity in the housing finance market. By their very mission, the two entities had a lot of power in determining which loans got issued in the first place: if Fannie Mae and Freddie Mac weren't willing to buy it, a loan was less likely to be made.

Unfortunately, though the CRA was pushing banks to make loans to a broader spectrum of borrowers, Fannie Mae and Freddie Mac were not keeping pace in terms of the loans they would buy. To conform to efforts in the primary market, Congress in 1992 established goals that required these two entities to serve lower income communities more actively.[7] In the late 1990s Fannie Mae made a trillion-dollar commitment to expanding lending services to underserved communities. By then it was clear not only that these services would make access to credit more equitable but also that investing in lower income home buyers was financially sound.

One of Fannie Mae's partners in learning this lesson was Self-Help Ventures Fund, an affiliate of Self-Help Credit Union, the nonprofit community development financial institution that Martin Eakes and Bonnie Wright founded in North Carolina in 1980. At that time, the median white American household had eleven times the net wealth of the median African American household, and Eakes and Wright had noticed that minorities and other disadvantaged households had unequal access to business loans.[8]

To address this racial wealth gap, they established Self-Help Ventures Fund. Their original intention was to make loans to small businesses and thereby create jobs and economic opportunity. But they soon discovered that one reason minority and lower resource entrepreneurs had less access to capital was that they did not enjoy an advantage that many well-off borrowers did—the ability to borrow against the equity in their homes.

Those involved with Self-Help Ventures Fund recognized that home equity constitutes a large share of household wealth, particularly among lower income households, and that homeowners had significantly more wealth than renters in the same income categories. In the late 1980s the wealth gap between owners and renters was substantial: the median homeowner's net worth was $120,000, while the median renter held just $2,400 in wealth.[9] Though homeownership is an important step in building wealth, at that time many people couldn't qualify for mortgages from mainstream banks.

Self-Help Credit Union (the institution with which Self-Help Ventures Fund is affiliated) began making carefully underwritten home loans directly to low-income and minority borrowers so they could gain the benefits of homeownership. Defaults proved very low, and within a few years the small lender started buying portfolios of community reinvestment mortgages originated under special programs from various North Carolina banks. Several of these banks would later grow through acquisitions and mergers until they stood among the nation's top ten. Because CRA performance factored heavily into regulators' decisions to allow bank mergers, these institutions were notably active in community mortgage lending.

These banks were making more mortgages to lower income communities, and though the loans were performing well, they did not meet the standards then in place for the secondary-market giants, Fannie Mae and Freddie Mac. Borrowers who qualified for community mortgage loans might have high debt-to-income ratios, limited assets, nontraditional employment, or nontraditional proof of creditworthiness. In addition, the loans often didn't require private mortgage insurance. The government-sponsored enterprises were unable to purchase these loans without additional risk assurances.

Though it had only $55 million in total assets at the time, in 1994 Self-Help acquired a $20 million CRA home loan portfolio from a North Carolina bank. In time, the nonprofit lender's track record convinced Fannie Mae, which by then was charged with meeting affordable housing goals, that mortgage loans to low-income borrowers were a good bet. The Self-Help model also highlighted the massive latent potential of private financial institutions to break down barriers to household economic security.

In 1998, with a $50 million grant from the Ford Foundation and institutional capacity provided by Fannie Mae, the Community Advantage Program (CAP) was launched. Under the program, Self-Help purchased community reinvestment loans from lenders and sold them to Fannie Mae, while retaining the associated risk. CAP had two purposes: to increase the flow of efficient, secondary-market capital to low-income and minority borrowers; and to demonstrate that making mortgages to these borrowers could be profitable for the lenders.

Between 1998 and 2009, CAP purchased over 46,000 loans made to low-income households, which were able to achieve homeownership and the benefits that go with it. CAP was one of several innovations being tested by Fannie Mae and Freddie Mac, to safely and sustainably expand homeownership opportunities.[10]

In the early 2000s, though, something else was changing in the mortgage market, and rapidly. People who had traditionally been shut out from financing and were beginning to gain access through innovations such as the CRA and a host of secondary-market innovations, of which CAP was one, were increasingly being offered a new kind of mortgage: subprime loans. These loans were largely unregulated and costly, but they provided people with the ability to buy or to refinance a home. These nontraditional, exotic loans included features that made them more complicated and riskier for borrowers than the traditional thirty-year, fixed-rate mortgage. And as the subsequent skyrocketing default rates of subprime and exotic mortgages demonstrate, these mortgage products did not provide the credit needed for sustained homeownership.

Nontraditional mortgages did not have Fannie Mae, Freddie Mac, or Ginnie Mae/FHA backing, and initially these mortgages represented a small part of the market. The loans were bundled into mortgage-backed securities and sold privately, outside of the traditional government-sponsored enterprises. But fed by a global oversupply of capital, the nontraditional mortgage and mortgage-backed security market grew explosively between 2003 and 2006, pumping out mortgage loans on the assumption that house prices would never stop going up. Easy money helped inflate the property value bubble, and rising home values kept credit readily available.

These unsustainable mortgages had features that would prove problematic: no documentation of income or assets, high upfront fees, risk-based pricing, prepayment penalties, teaser rates, balloon payments, and negative amortization. Borrowers and the investors who bought these mortgages from the initial lenders took on risks that they did not understand and, more perilous for the economy, that they ultimately could not bear. Meanwhile, those who issued the loans made large, short-term profits. Eventually, Fannie Mae and Freddie Mac began to invest in these subprime loans and private label securities, which gave the practices legitimacy and momentum. Though community groups, housing advocates, and regulators in several states called for this unregulated sector to be reined in, federal regulators instead hailed such practices as innovations.

In late 2007 delinquency rates in the subprime and the riskier-than-prime Alternative A (Alt-A) sectors began to skyrocket.[11] Financial institutions failed, leading to a credit freeze. The U.S. mortgage market—once the envy of the world because it made economic opportunity available to so many—was a shambles. The government put the mortgage market on life support in 2008 by taking Fannie Mae and Freddie Mac into conservatorship and turned to the FHA once again to lead the way forward: in 2010, nine out of every ten U.S. mortgages were purchased by the government-sponsored enterprises or insured by the FHA. In contrast, the private sector response to the crisis has been to retrench and tighten underwriting guidelines. In fact, private lending all but shut down.

What should be the long-term response to the mortgage crisis? In July 2010 President Obama signed financial reform legislation, the Dodd-Frank Wall Street Reform and Consumer Protection Act (Dodd-Frank Act). The comprehensive legislation is structured to promote a return to safety and soundness in financial markets and to curb those behaviors that led to the crisis. The act promotes financial stability, improves accountability and transparency, discourages corporations from becoming "too big to fail," and protects consumers from abusive financial practices. The ultimate effect of the law will not be known for some time, since the process of rulemaking is far from complete. However, we do know what is not in the act: an explicit overview of how credit for affordable homeownership should become available again. Clearly, policymakers should take the invaluable lessons learned from the mortgage lending debacle and do better. But how?

Our research aims to answer this question. Through exhaustive examination of a Community Reinvestment Act loan portfolio, we set out to discern precisely what has and what hasn't worked in the affordable mortgage lending industry. We do so in order to provide policymakers and legislators with the best possible information as they work to strengthen the financial system without unreasonably restricting access to credit. In this book, we share what we know and make recommendations for an equitable, sustainable homeownership policy.

Until now, policymakers have had little in the way of real-time data with which to chart their course. However, the Center for Community Capital at the University of North Carolina at Chapel Hill has tracked mortgage loans made to lower income borrowers since 1999 to see whether this lending meets sound business criteria. The borrowers the center is following started with low net worth, low incomes, and low credit scores or no credit history at all (as is the case for recent immigrants to this country, for instance). Obviously, borrowers who have fewer resources pose a higher risk than borrowers with greater resources, since a borrower with more resources can tap into those resources in times of crisis. But does the fact of their having limited resources mean borrowers with low incomes are too risky to lend to?

The issue, center researchers discovered, is not whether low-income, low-resource individuals pose a greater risk than those with higher incomes. It is that the nature of the mortgage they receive can either amplify or mitigate that risk. The depth of our data allows us to examine this thoroughly, and we find that the wrong mortgage product exacerbates some risk characteristics. Our unique analysis provides important evidence as to the benefits and pitfalls of homeownership for a population traditionally underserved by the mainstream market. More telling, the timing of our study (with data gathered from 2003 to the present) allows us to examine these benefits and pitfalls in times of both boom and bust. As we detail in the chapters that follow, our analysis demonstrates that correctly structured loans to low-income households perform quite well: it is indeed possible to regain the dream of homeownership while minimizing the risk that doing so will result in another economic nightmare.

In chapter 2 we explore the value of homeownership, illustrate how it has benefited the middle class, and trace how government policy has shaped the housing finance system. We describe more fully how affordable lending programs strive to make these benefits accessible to more working families, and we argue that community reinvestment lending has been consistent with safe and sound financial principles. Where it occurs, this type of lending is doing what it was designed to do: promote fair access, choice, and prosperity in low-income and minority communities while profiting financial institutions.

In chapter 3 we differentiate between community reinvestment lending that increases access to sustainable credit for lower income borrowers and the reckless lending that led to the foreclosure crisis and devastated families and communities. We examine the evolution and the results of the shadow mortgage system, identifying the regulatory failures, speculation, and faulty products that resulted in economic meltdown.

Then in chapter 4 we look at what happens when lending is done right. Community Advantage Program mortgages have significantly lower rates of default and prepayment than subprime loans. To determine why, we examined the performance of more than 46,000 CAP loans and conducted in-depth interviews on the long-term effects of affordable homeownership. We also compared outcomes for CAP borrowers and subprime borrowers in the same communities. Based on our findings, we pinpoint the practices that caused harm and those that created the greatest possible benefits both for the mortgage industry and for low- and moderate-income homeowners.

Chapter 5 distills the lessons we are learning about borrowers and their experiences during the financial crisis. We examine how CAP borrowers are managing during the Great Recession. In particular, we examine the financial and psychological stressors they are facing and how these owners are coping during tumultuous economic times.

In chapter 6 we turn to the question of how we can ensure that lower income individuals who both desire and are willing to work for homeownership can purchase a home and remain in that home as long as they want to. In this chapter, we glean lessons from the analysis presented in chapters 4 and 5, and we suggest changes to lending practices that will enable and extend low-income and minority homeownership moving forward. We concentrate on four areas: product design, underwriting, origination, and servicing.

In chapter 7 we turn to the issue of what factors would be necessary to bring community reinvestment lending to scale nationally. We look at three things in particular: the credit enhancement mechanism that enabled the Community Advantage Program, the functions of the secondary market that allow the program to thrive, and the broader systemic stability required for affordable home lending to take place.

In the book's final chapter, we turn to the core elements of a housing finance policy that will enable all sound mortgage lending going forward. To be effective, we argue, housing finance and regulatory policy must promote well-functioning markets, encourage the appropriate use of technological innovation, align the interests of market participants, minimize potential conflicts of interest, and guarantee the well-being of consumers in the mortgage marketplace. Only with these supports will America's housing finance market be strengthened to fulfill its original purpose—that of giving all Americans who are able and willing to work for homeownership a fair opportunity to have access to sustainable mortgage loans and the foundations of prosperity.

Important as that goal is, homeownership policy that works must do more than expand the universe of people eligible for mortgage products. It must also address the loan products themselves and ensure that they are sound investments for both mortgage lenders and borrowers. The evidence is clear that good lending programs create profit for the loan industry and successfully expand access to credit for underserved communities. Lending that follows the community reinvestment model has proved to be sustainable, and it has had excellent economic and social results.

But those results can be improved. Every market participant, whether private or public, regulator or regulated, shares some culpability for the mortgage finance crisis, and we recommend ways to prevent future missteps. It is not enough to make mortgages. The country must work to enhance the ability of those who take out those mortgages to stay in their homes over the long term.

In responding to the mortgage crisis, it is essential to protect and improve fair access to homeownership opportunities and the social and economic benefits those opportunities provide. The chapters that follow detail our findings on how these goals can be achieved.

2

Promoting Sound, Equitable Homeownership

Since America's founding, owning property has been considered the distinctive characteristic of full citizenship. In twelve of the original thirteen states, only property-owning white males could vote, a requirement that restricted the franchise to 10 percent of the adult population. Moreover, the majority of those who could vote couldn't hold an elected position because they didn't own enough property. Similarly, in many states, only property owners could sit on juries and engage in other civic activities.

As the American democracy matured, the property-owning requirements for full civic participation slowly disappeared, and owning one's home became seen as a civic virtue instead.[1] As a virtue, homeownership demonstrated that a person's life and conduct conformed to the moral and ethical principles many believed defined the American character. Owning a home is a future-oriented activity and so is implicitly optimistic. Homeownership signals thrift and an intention to provide for one's own needs. Buying a home signifies responsibility and a willingness to commit to something larger than oneself—a specific neighborhood or community. Over time, the belief emerged that homeownership didn't just reflect but rather engendered these desirable attributes.

For much of U.S. history, national leaders put this belief into practice by promoting homeownership. This happened as far back as 1862, when Abraham Lincoln signed the Homestead Act, giving applicants title to 160 acres of undeveloped land outside of the original thirteen colonies. Presidents since Hoover have all emphasized and supported homeownership as a means for achieving financial stability and security. They believed that homeownership was beneficial for individuals and communities.

Recent research shows that homeownership does indeed have individual benefits, particularly financial ones. Homes give their owners not only shelter but also an opportunity to build wealth. Owning a home helps people build wealth in two ways: it forces them to save by paying down the principal owed, and it increases their net worth when the house appreciates beyond the cost of the down payment and mortgage. In this way, homeowners can increase their wealth by investing borrowed funds. Since 1913 the United States has subsidized the home as an investment by allowing homeowners to deduct the mortgage interest and property tax they pay on their homes; the bigger the mortgage, the bigger the deduction. In 2012 the mortgage interest deduction is expected to cost the federal treasury about $131 billion and the property tax deduction about $31 billion. In addition, homeowners are expected to save about $50 billion due to the exclusion of tax on the first $250,000 ($500,000 for joint returns) of capital gains on housing.[2] Not surprisingly, those who earn the most get the most benefit from these subsidies.[3]

The home as an investment has come to represent a significant fraction of household wealth, especially for lower income people. The Joint Center for Housing Studies finds that home equity makes up 55 percent of the wealth of the median minority homeowner and represents close to 80 percent of the wealth of the median owner with income below $20,000. The same study finds that home equity is close to half of the wealth of the median sixty-five-to-seventy-four-year-old owner, thus composing a critical postretirement resource.[4]

Research also demonstrates that homeownership benefits communities. Homeowners tend to be more involved in a wide range of neighborhood-based activities. They are less mobile than comparable renters.[5] Neighborhoods with high homeownership rates have more stability and less turnover than those made up mostly of renters. Even when we account for neighborhood conditions, homeowners are more likely to participate in neighborhood organizations and to vote in local elections.[6] They are more likely to know neighbors who can help with tasks such as building a deck or fixing a computer.[7]

If there are individual and community-level benefits associated with homeownership, then it follows logically that government policy that promotes homeownership is by definition policy that distributes these benefits. While fairness would require that the opportunity to own a home be spread equitably, a quick look at how U.S. housing finance policy has evolved makes clear that a fair distribution of the benefits of homeownership has not always been a central goal of this policy.

Government Policy and the Shaping of the Housing Finance System

The federal government radically transformed the American financial system during the Great Depression of the 1930s, when new policies were put into place in response to a financial crisis. The goal was not necessarily to encourage homeownership, yet as these policies evolved, they did just that. Housing economists Richard Green and Susan Wachter trace this evolution, and we recap their findings here.[8]

Before the 1930s the mortgage market was a purely private industry. Most mortgages required down payments of 50 percent. These were short-term loans with balloon payments and variable interest rates. Borrowers had to refinance periodically, something they could do because property values continued to rise. During the 1930s, when property values declined by half, many borrowers were unable to refinance and pay back their mortgages. A wave of foreclosures ensued, further depressing housing values and exacerbating the crisis.

The government responded decisively by intervening in the housing finance system. In just three years (1932–34) lawmakers created three important institutions: the Federal Home Loan Bank (FHLB) system, the Home Owner's Loan Corporation (HOLC), and the Federal Housing Administration (FHA). The FHLB, a collection of regional cooperative banks from which banks obtain low-cost funds to lend for housing and economic development, was created to increase liquidity for new loans. To stem the spread of foreclosures, the HOLC purchased about a million defaulted mortgages from financial institutions and converted them into fixed-rate, long-term, fully amortizing mortgages. The government established the FHA to provide the mortgage insurance necessary, in the form of a full guaranty, to give lenders confidence to make mortgages. Together, these agencies allowed financial institutions that had lost liquidity in the crisis to start making mortgage loans again.

Lawmakers terminated the HOLC in 1936 and in 1938 set up a new agency to provide a secondary-market outlet for FHA-insured loans: the Federal National Mortgage Association (Fannie Mae). Fannie Mae purchased loans originated by primary lenders. It borrowed money from the debt markets, traditionally at a rate much lower than other banks due to the government guarantee implied in its federal charter, and used the funds to buy mortgages as its own investments. Through this mechanism, Fannie Mae injected new money into the housing economy.[9] Eventually, in 1981, the agency issued its first mortgage-backed securities.[10]

In the closing years of World War II, both to reward veterans and to stimulate the housing market, the federal government established the Veterans' Administration (VA) as part of the GI Bill. The VA mortgage program allowed returning veterans to obtain mortgages with low down payments. At about the same time, in an effort to promote housing construction, the FHA liberalized its mortgage insurance requirements. In 1948 the agency extended the maximum term for a mortgage it would insure to thirty years. Eight years later, it raised the maximum loan-to-value ratio to 95 percent for new homes and to 90 percent for existing homes. The FHA retained a cap on the size of the loans it insured, which allowed the private sector to develop a mortgage insurance market for high balance loans.

Government policies not only changed the type of mortgages that undergirded the American dream, they also changed who provided capital for those mortgages. Starting in the 1930s the U.S. government guaranteed deposits through the Federal Deposit Insurance Corporation (FDIC) system. Consequently, depository institutions—banks and savings and loans—could raise capital from depositors, who were attracted by higher yields than investors could earn with treasury bonds. Depository institutions, especially savings and loans (S&Ls), became the major sources of mortgage funds for about two decades.

Consequently, government policy induced the for-profit private sector to resume a major role in the mortgage market. This time, private lenders—mostly S&Ls—developed products similar to those offered by the FHA: fixed-rate, self-amortizing, privately insured mortgages. Over time, the private sector share of the mortgage market grew and the FHA share declined, from almost 30 percent in 1970 to less than 10 percent in the mid-1990s.

As Green and Wachter explain, inflation spikes, which started in the mid-1960s and led to volatile and rising interest rates, shattered this funding mechanism for mortgages. Because of government policy, depository institutions had caps on the interest rate they paid depositors. As a result, people moved their deposits from S&Ls to treasury bonds and to higher yielding alternative savings vehicles such as money market funds, mutual funds, and pension funds. Despite their government backing, suddenly the S&Ls had a liquidity problem they couldn't fix. To attract deposits, they would have to pay more, but to do so, they would have to raise the interest rates on the mortgages they made with those deposits.

Unfortunately, the S&Ls' lending capital was locked up in the low-rate, long-term mortgages they already had on their balance sheets. This mismatch between short-term, rate-sensitive funding and long-term, fixed-rate lending laid the foundation for the S&L crisis of the 1980s and 1990s.[11] Congress responded by relaxing so many of the restrictions on these institutions that many pursued reckless strategies, ultimately leading to a massive taxpayer-backed bailout.

Policymakers responded to the housing finance liquidity crisis of the 1960s and 1970s in other ways. To foster an alternative channel for mortgage finance, they first split Fannie Mae into two agencies in 1968: the Government National Mortgage Association (Ginnie Mae), which would focus on FHA-backed loans, and a new Fannie Mae, now a privately held company that could buy and sell nongovernment-backed mortgages and so increase liquidity in the rest of the market. In 1970 the federal government created the Federal Home Loan Mortgage Corporation (Freddie Mac) to provide a secondary-market outlet to the savings and loan sector. In creating Ginnie Mae, the new Fannie Mae, and Freddie Mac, lawmakers intended to avoid future liquidity problems and to standardize the mortgage market.

The policy response to the liquidity crisis dramatically transformed the housing finance system. Even after the federal government removed deposit ceilings and began to allow adjustable-rate mortgages (ARMs) in 1982, depository institutions continued to shy away from holding onto fixed-rate loans out of fear of inflation. Instead, lenders sold most fixed-rate loans they originated to Fannie Mae, Freddie Mac, or Ginnie Mae. The agencies then packaged these mortgages into mortgage-backed securities, which they sold to investors who could hold long-term assets with fixed rates. This so-called securitization process has supplied most of the mortgage funds in the United States ever since, as Wall Street adapted the government's model in order to securitize larger loans (known as jumbo loans) that Fannie, Freddie, and Ginnie were not allowed to purchase.

Increasingly, middle- and high-income American households were enjoying low-cost, low-risk mortgages with modest fixed rates and a free right to prepay if a lower rate loan became available. Borrowers all over the country could open their Sunday paper and compare prices on a standard, thirty-year, fixed-rate mortgage. They knew exactly what they were getting and didn't have to worry too much about the fine print. Likewise, investors all over the world could buy safe and sound mortgage-backed securities issued by Fannie Mae and Freddie Mac, which, because of their federal charter, were believed to carry the full faith and confidence, or at least the implied backing, of the U.S. government. They too knew what they were getting and didn't have to read the fine print. How did this situation come about?

The short answer is that a series of government initiatives supported the necessary capital market developments. The longer, more technical answer has three parts. First, lending risks were shifted from the lenders who made the loans (the primary market) to the secondary market—that is, to the investors who bought the loans once they had been packaged into mortgage-backed securities. Second, investors dissipated interest rate risk by hedging and buying just those mortgage-backed securities that met their cash flow needs. Third, FHA, Ginnie Mae, Fannie Mae, Freddie Mac, and in some cases the private mortgage insurance market absorbed the credit risk; these institutions also guaranteed payment to investors in case loans went bad.

By shifting around the risks associated with mortgage lending, federal policy gave nondepository institutions (such as mortgage banks) a way to play a major role in originating mortgages. It also allowed these players to attract a much larger pool of capital than the depositories had at their disposal. Although government policy gradually shifted mortgage activity and risk away from federally backed depositories and toward mortgage banks and secondary-market players, by the very fact of designing the policy and implicitly backing the activity, the U.S. government was still heavily involved in shaping and supporting the American mortgage market.

Inequitable Results of U.S Housing Policy

Government policy was the catalyst that caused the private housing finance sector to flourish and allowed families to enjoy the financial and social benefits of homeownership with safe mortgage products. For decades, however, that policy also promoted a structure that restricted enjoyment of these benefits disproportionally to high-income, white households. How is it that these advantages were not distributed equally throughout society? Again, a brief history helps to answer this question.

When it began to assume the risks for mortgage lending during the Great Depression, the federal government needed to quantify these risks. Toward this end, the HOLC, established by Congress in 1933, developed appraisal practices and standards that may well have been the beginning of redlining in the United States.[12] HOLC appraisers collected information on urban real estate and created a rating system that undervalued dense, mixed, or aging neighborhoods. By definition, this rating system undervalued central city neighborhoods while working in favor of newer suburban developments.

Government practices also led to discrimination against minority borrowers and neighborhoods. As surprising as it may seem today, in the early 1900s most urban African Americans lived in neighborhoods that were predominantly white. This did not remain the case, however. Those informing federal policy believed that integrated neighborhoods had unstable property values, and the federal government began to advocate for the preservation of all-white neighborhoods. Toward this end, until they were ruled unenforceable in 1948, the FHA required that there be racially restrictive covenants on the properties it insured.[13] In addition, the FHA advised in its *Underwriting Manual* (1938) that "if a neighborhood is to retain stability, it is necessary that properties shall continue to be occupied by the same social and racial classes. A change in social or racial occupancy generally contributes to instability and a decline in values."[14]

These federal policies and practices were similar to the policies and practices of private institutions in the real estate industry. For example, the National Association of Real Estate Boards' national code of ethics for the years 1924 to 1950 states that "a realtor should never be instrumental in introducing into a neighborhood a character of property or occupancy, members of any race or nationality, or any individual whose presence will clearly be detrimental to property values in the neighborhood."[15] Similarly, the 1935 text of the American Institute of Real Estate Appraisers warned appraisers to consider the effects of the "infiltration of inharmonious racial groups" when assessing the value of a property.[16]

The combination of these policies and practices helped support the creation of economically healthy white suburbs and economically struggling, primarily minority, central cities. If dense, aging, and mixed development was considered less valuable, central city areas by definition would be undervalued. If it was important to keep racial and social stability in neighborhoods, then as white middle-class people were the first occupants of new suburban developments, black Americans would find themselves excluded from these areas. The effects of these policies are apparent in the distribution of FHA-backed mortgages, which until the 1960s went mainly to white suburban home buyers. Between 1934 and 1959, FHA supported 60 percent of home purchases. Between the mid-1940s and mid-1950s, only 2 percent of these mortgages went to black Americans.

Over several decades, then, government policies encouraged the suburbanization of America at the expense of urban areas. The housing finance system and the housing market, often bolstered by local regulations, incorporated these practices. As a result, redlining was officially sanctioned, and mortgage lending in minority, mixed-race, and ethnic areas was limited for many years.

Creating Broader Access to Housing Finance

Despite the 1948 Supreme Court ruling that racially restrictive covenants could not be enforced, market participants continued to do business in a way that perpetuated pre-1948 patterns of lending and development. It was only in 1968 that the Supreme Court held that federal law bars all racial discrimination (private or public) in the sale or rental of property. However, by the mid-1970s it became clear that the credit needed to purchase a home and benefit from homeownership was still not available to all creditworthy Americans. What would it take to address this market failure and undo patterns of behavior developed over many decades? Once again, it took government intervention.

Over time, three prototypes of government intervention emerged. Under the fully public model, a government agency channels capital from global markets to the nation's housing market, generally to serve those unable to borrow from the mainstream financial system. To take one example, Ginnie Mae is an agency of the federal government, located within the U.S. Department of Housing and Urban Development. Ginnie Mae does not buy or sell loans, nor does it issue mortgage-backed securities. Instead, it guarantees investors the timely payment of principal and interest on securities backed by federally insured or guaranteed mortgage loans. The Ginnie Mae guarantee allows lenders to obtain a better price for their mortgage loans in the secondary market. Lenders can then use the proceeds to make new loans.[17] Historically, Ginnie Mae securities are the only mortgage-backed securities that carry the full explicit guaranty of the U.S. government—in other words, the commitment that the government will make good on the underlying debt. Under this model, the federal government facilitates the extension of affordable mortgage credit, a public benefit, while at the same time carrying all the risks.

Under a hybrid public/private model, the government creates entities charged in part with pursuing a public purpose, such as the extension of credit to underserved markets. The government-sponsored enterprises (GSEs) are examples of the public/private model. The GSEs are corporations (that is, privately owned, for-profit firms) that are federally chartered for a public purpose. Congress created the GSEs to improve market efficiency and to overcome statutory and market imperfections that otherwise prevented funds from moving easily to those who needed them. Congress grants the GSEs benefits and privileges while requiring them to promote selected public policy objectives. Before considering the third model of government intervention, we pause to look further at the GSEs.

Five GSEs are part of the housing finance system. Fannie Mae, Freddie Mac, and the Federal Agricultural Mortgage Corporation (Farmer Mac) are investor owned. In contrast, member institutions own cooperatively the Federal Home Loan Bank system and the Farm Credit System. Broadly speaking, the GSEs have the power to issue loans or loan guarantees for limited purposes. They raise funds by borrowing, but their debts normally do not carry the full faith and credit of the federal government.[18]

There are some notable differences in the way the various GSEs operate. Fannie Mae and Freddie Mac's main purpose is to generate a flow of funds from capital markets for mortgages. Farmer Mac is a stockholder-owned company chartered in 1988 to serve as a secondary market in agricultural loans, agricultural real estate, and rural housing. The Federal Home Loan Bank system, created in 1932, provides stable, on-demand, low-cost funding to financial institutions for home mortgage, small business, rural development, and economic development lending. The system, with its twelve banks owned by over 8,100 regulated financial institutions, is the largest collective source of home mortgage and community credit in the country. The Farm Credit System, established in 1916, is a chartered network of cooperatives and related service organizations that lends to agricultural producers, rural homeowners, and other farm-related businesses.

Although privately owned, Fannie Mae and Freddie Mac have benefited financially from their public/private nature. By statute, the securities issued by these two entities must contain a disclaimer that they are not guaranteed by, and do not constitute debt or obligation of, the United States. Despite the disclaimer, Wall Street and investors worldwide have believed that the federal government would rescue Fannie and Freddie if they were to become insolvent. The two institutions were able to borrow money at significantly lower costs than their competitors because of this belief.[19] Although some of these benefits have translated into lower interest rates for borrowers, critics of the hybrid model have expressed concerns that the subsidy is more likely to end up benefiting stock and bond holders and top management in the companies.[20]

The third model of government intervention is that within which private institutions that serve a public purpose and receive a public benefit either agree or are required to meet public goals. The 1977 Community Reinvestment Act (CRA) is an example of such an intervention. Under the act, banks are required to meet the public goal of extending sustainable credit in an equitable manner; the rationale for their doing so is that they receive benefits (deposit insurance, subsidies from the Federal Reserve system) that are subsidized by the public. Banks' compliance with the act is assessed using data gathered under the 1975 Home Mortgage Disclosure Act (HMDA). Under HMDA, lenders must file an annual, loan-level report on the characteristics of all mortgages they make; this reporting includes the race and income of the borrower and the neighborhood in which the home is located. HMDA data have played a key role in assessing community lending activities under the CRA.

The CRA was a critical factor in the expansion of low-cost, low-risk credit to more Americans. It encouraged federally insured banks and thrifts to meet the financial needs throughout the regions in which they operate, including low- and moderate-income areas. The legislation exhorted lenders to create access to credit in underserved neighborhoods but stipulated that such lending should remain consistent with banks' safe and sound operation. In other words, it directly instructed lenders to meet the financial needs of creditworthy borrowers but recognized that individual lenders should determine the extent and characteristics of such lending according to the circumstances in which they operate.

Although it is not focused solely on housing finance, the CRA has expanded access to sustainable mortgages with the same terms and conditions that made homeownership so beneficial for higher income groups. Lenders have extended mainstream products that combine traditional risk management techniques with local knowledge. At the time the CRA was enacted, banks were located in the communities where the loans were made, and they often lent to people who were already customers and whose loans they could thus monitor closely. Because they were directly involved with borrowers and with the community, lenders had the additional information they needed to make sustainable loans that remote secondary-market and private mortgage insurance institutions considered too risky.

Progress in broadening access to credit was slow, however. A 1992 study by the Federal Reserve Bank of Boston documents that minority mortgage applicants in the Boston area were 56 percent more likely to be turned down than were equivalent white applicants.[21] The study combined HMDA data with loan, property, neighborhood, and applicant characteristics, including credit history information. The study was subject to intense criticism, yet its conclusions remain valid because no other study has ever incorporated such complete data.

In the 1990s prime lenders improved their ability to observe and quantify risk through new computer-based technologies, which encouraged them to experiment with flexible underwriting and develop targeted lending programs.[22] Many lenders created special low-risk, fixed-rate mortgage products that allowed lower down payments, lower credit scores or alternative proof of creditworthiness, higher housing expenditures and total debt burdens, and similar features that put home-ownership within reach of more low-income, low-wealth borrowers.

But because of their flexible underwriting, these community rein-vestment products often did not meet secondary-market requirements: Fannie Mae, Freddie Mac, and other investors considered them too risky to buy. As a result, the originating lender had to keep them in portfolio. Because these affordable loans tied up capital, lenders nor-mally set a limit on how many they were willing to issue. Researchers have estimated that CRA-related programs originated only 20,000 to 30,000 loans a year.[23]

It became clear that CRA-related lending was going to remain lim-ited unless there developed a secondary market for affordable home loans. Since 1992 the federal government has required Fannie Mae and Freddie Mac to invest more in the emerging community reinvestment market, thereby making more capital available for new loans. The 1992 Federal Housing Enterprises Financial Safety and Soundness Act required the two agencies to meet certain affordable housing targets, though these new goals didn't line up with CRA goals. The CRA counts loans that a lender makes within its assessment area either to borrowers who have 80 percent or less of the median area income or in census tracts where the median income is 80 percent or less of the area median income. Fannie Mae and Freddie Mac's affordable hous-ing goals are satisfied by a range of criteria, including income and racial makeup of borrowers and neighborhoods; in some cases bor-rower income can be as high as 120 percent of area median income.

Despite the imperfect alignment of goals, Fannie Mae and Freddie Mac were slowly but surely starting to buy more CRA products from banks and so were moving, on their own, toward greater support of affordable home lending. Moreover, they were responding to pressure from banks to purchase their whole spectrum of loans.

Still, several studies in the mid- and late 1990s claim that Fannie Mae and Freddie Mac were lagging the market in their service. By comparing the characteristics of loans originated by other lenders to the characteristics of mortgages purchased by the GSEs, the studies claim that the two agencies weren't buying enough loans to meet the demand of community reinvestment lenders.[24]

The Next Frontier:
A Secondary Market for Community Reinvestment Loans

To address this disconnect, Self-Help established the Community Advantage Program (CAP) in 1998 with funding from the Ford Foundation and in partnership with Fannie Mae. Created to connect community reinvestment loans with the secondary market, CAP made it easier for Fannie Mae to serve the low- and moderate-income market. Through the creation of CAP, Self-Help had a significant role in bringing the secondary housing market into community reinvestment lending.

CAP has its roots in Self-Help's own mortgage lending, which dates back to the mid-1980s. Though an active community development lender, Self-Help understood that, as a relatively small credit union, it could make only a limited number of loans. By the early 1990s, motivated in part by the CRA, banks were using their branching networks to originate a significant volume of home loans to lower wealth families. Without a secondary market for these loans, however, banks had to hold them on their books. As a result, banks had limited capital available to lend and thus capped the number of nonconforming loans they would make.

In an effort to increase affordable home lending by addressing these constraints, in 1994 Self-Help pulled together funding to purchase a $20 million mortgage loan portfolio from Wachovia Bank in North Carolina; Wachovia agreed to use the proceeds from the sale to originate another $20 million in nonconforming loans. Self-Help's lending experience had led it to conclude that loans made to low- and moderate-income families would perform well and were worth the gamble in order to help create a small secondary market for nonconforming loans. That first transaction was successful and performed well. Over the next few years Self-Help went on to undertake a series of secondary-market transactions with other North Carolina banks.

Banks in North Carolina would soon prove to have an advantage over banks elsewhere because the state's banking laws had long allowed for branch banking. When the Riegle-Neal Interstate Banking and Branching Efficiency Act of 1994 passed, banks all over the country began to acquire banks in other states, and a huge wave of consolidation followed. In the early 1990s North Carolina's banks tended to be stronger and bigger than banks in other states and so were in a better position to make interstate acquisitions.

But like banks everywhere, North Carolina's banks had a hurdle to overcome. The CRA required banks that wanted approval for their mergers and acquisitions to demonstrate strong CRA performance. Meeting these performance standards became an important means by which banks could show that they were indeed serving the communities in which they did business. As was the case for banks elsewhere, North Carolina's banks had undertaken CRA mortgage lending, but because the programs they offered had exceptions to standard underwriting guidelines, Fannie Mae and Freddie Mac wouldn't buy those loans. Eager to expand, the banks needed to sell their CRA loans in order to issue new affordable loans, yet at that point there was nowhere to sell them.

Self-Help's original Wachovia purchase and ensuing purchases in North Carolina, which by 1998 totaled $100 million, were performing very well. Self-Help shared its results and plans with Fannie Mae and with the Ford Foundation. The latter was so impressed that in 1998 it gave what was at the time the largest grant ever made to promote homeownership: $50 million to Self-Help Ventures Fund to create the Community Advantage Program for low- and moderate-income families. In essence, the Ford Foundation grant strengthened Self-Help's capital base so that it could purchase affordable home loans from lenders and then work with Fannie Mae to securitize the loans, using the Ford grant as recourse against losses. Fannie Mae was willing to securitize and buy these loans because Self-Help agreed to hold all the credit risk. Initially, the goal was for Self-Help to back and Fannie Mae to buy $2 billion worth of mortgages over a five-year period.

CAP began with five lenders: NationsBank, Bank of America, Norwest, Chase, and Bank One. By 2003 twenty-nine institutions from across the country were selling their affordable mortgages to Self-Help. Participants included banks, credit unions, mortgage companies, and nonprofit community development financial institutions. Some smaller, regional lenders used Self-Help as their exclusive outlet for their CRA loans, while bigger lenders sold only some of their loans through CAP.

These loans are generally purchase money, thirty-year, fixed-rate mortgages that are retail originated—that is, not made through a broker. Both Self-Help and Fannie Mae apply general underwriting standards; they also review and approve lenders' proposed program guidelines. By and large, however, lenders design their loan programs according to their own needs. Some lenders require prepurchase counseling; others don't. Loan-to-value ratios are set by the lenders but must be approved by Self-Help and Fannie Mae. And although Self-Help encourages lenders to offer postpurchase intervention in case borrowers encounter difficulties making their payments, not all lenders do so.

Self-Help retains recourse for the loans, meaning that if a loan defaults, Self-Help bears the loss and pays the cost. (Interestingly, selling loans with recourse was once such a common practice among banks that it was known as "the regular option.") Fannie Mae sells the loans to investors in the form of mortgage-backed securities or holds the loans in its own portfolio. Consequently, Self-Help needs only a relatively small staff to manage these transactions.

CAP has dramatically expanded homeownership. When CAP met its original five-year goal of $2 billion in loans in 2003, Fannie Mae set a new goal of $4 billion. The program has met this further goal and continues to provide an impressive demonstration of the power of leverage. Had Ford's $50 million been used solely to make mortgages, the money would have enabled only 633 lower income families to become owners.[25] By using the $50 million for credit enhancement, CAP created a multiplier effect, which has supported 46,000 owners in affordable homeownership. And by creating a bridge between the primary and secondary markets for these loans, CAP helped expand the availability of fairly priced loans to lower income, first-time homebuyers.

CAP's lending guidelines were bold by the standards of the time, though the market would adopt much riskier guidelines by the mid-2000s. Under CAP, lenders offered loan-to-value ratios of 95 to 103 percent and flexible ways of considering a borrower's credit and income. But most lenders had to underwrite each and every loan; Self-Help would generally not buy loans originated by brokers, and through most of the program's history the lender was liable for losses for the first year after each loan originated. This final stipulation—that is, if a borrower defaulted in the first twelve months Self-Help would give the loan back to the lender—ensured that lenders took adequate care in the approval process. Lenders can sell newly originated loans to CAP on a loan-by-loan basis (a "flow" basis), or they can sell in a lump sum previously originated, active loans that they have been holding in portfolio. Self-Help will not buy any existing loans that are delinquent or have had a recent delinquency.

How CAP Performs in Real Life

The Community Advantage Program provides a unique opportunity for evaluating the benefits and costs of affordable mortgage lending for both homeowners and mortgage lenders. Once CAP was up and running successfully, the Ford Foundation called on the Center for Community Capital to evaluate the program. In 1999, the center began a longitudinal study to determine whether loans made through CAP posed a reasonable degree of risk and whether the program could and should be replicated. In addition, we set out to see whether Fannie Mae and Freddie Mac should buy affordable home loans without Self-Help acting as the middleman.

We also realized that the unique information we were gathering would allow us to measure the impact of homeownership on low-income families, something that had not previously been studied with a national sample of borrowers. Our project has turned out to provide an additional, unexpected opportunity—it is letting us learn about the experiences of lower income homeowners not just during the housing boom but also during the worst housing market conditions in decades.

What we're learning provides the basis for this book. For more than a decade now we have been gathering information on loan origination and on loan performance over time, information we combine with data from an ongoing, in-depth annual borrower survey. Because we conduct these longitudinal studies simultaneously, we can link what happens in a borrower's life to what happens to his or her mortgage. Until now, when analysts have debated the importance of certain factors in loan performance, they have generally lacked concrete information about what actually happens to the borrowers or the loans after origination. They didn't know how borrowers' situations change over time—how their income and employment change, or how their finances are affected if they get divorced or sick or lose their jobs. We are collecting the data necessary to test the effect of events like these on the ability of low-income homeowners to retain their homes.

Before we undertook our project, those of us who study homeownership lacked information on how individual property values change over time. We might have information about a home's value when the mortgage originated, or we might ask a borrower how much his or her home is worth today, but we didn't have outside corroboration on these figures. The CAP study provides this information because we collect Fannie Mae's estimates of current property values every quarter. We also gather real-time information on participants' credit scores.

Just Who Are CAP's Borrowers?

CAP's borrowers have a median annual household income of $30,792.[26] Just under a third of them bought homes in low-income census tracts. The median loan balance at origination for CAP's borrowers was $79,000, and this amount was issued at an interest rate of 7.25 percent. Forty-four percent of CAP's borrowers had credit scores less than or equal to 660 when their mortgages were originated, and close to 70 percent of borrowers made less than a 5 percent down payment on their homes.

CAP's borrowers are concentrated in the southeastern United States and tend to live in more developed regions, with only 14 percent living in rural areas. The median borrower is thirty-two years old. Some 41 percent of CAP borrower households are headed by a woman, and almost half of CAP's borrowers have children living in the home. Approximately 61 percent of CAP's borrowers are white, 58 percent are married or in a committed relationship, and 88 percent have at least a high school diploma.

CAP has enabled a group of creditworthy, though nontraditional, borrowers to obtain homes with thirty-year, fixed-rate mortgages. Roughly 90 percent of CAP's borrowers failed to meet at least one of the three traditional lending criteria: a loan-to-value ratio less than or equal to 90 percent, a debt-to-income ratio less than or equal to 38 percent, and a credit score of 640 or greater. While 59 percent of CAP's borrowers met two out of three of these criteria and therefore might have qualified for a loan from a mainstream institution with some additional scrutiny, they were in fact unable to obtain such a loan. CAP's participating lenders took these creditworthy borrowers and worked with them to get them into homes they could afford with mortgages they could manage.

How does CAP stimulate lending to lower income people? When a lender sells a portfolio of previously originated loans to CAP, it commits to relend the same amount to similar borrowers. One facet of our investigation was to determine whether CAP in fact increased the liquidity of nonstandard community reinvestment loans by permanently expanding the secondary mortgage market. We find that it has. From 1998 to 2009 CAP helped finance the purchase of over 46,000 home loans to low-income and minority borrowers from thirty-eight lenders in forty-eight states. The loans total more than $4.5 billion; they were purchased and then sold in the secondary market.

Comparing CAP and Subprime Loans

The explosion of subprime lending and the subsequent financial crisis highlight the importance of lending in a sound, responsible way. When the subprime mortgage crisis hit, we began to understand that our data have the potential to show the market not just how to expand but also how to lend in a way that is sustainable for both borrowers and lending institutions. We saw that we had in our hands information that could help the market move forward safely.

The CAP data allow us to answer certain questions related to the mortgage crisis. One of these questions is whether lending to low-income/minority borrowers caused the mortgage meltdown. Because we can track the relative impact of such factors as mortgage terms, credit scores, property values, and employment status, we can show that it was not risky borrowers but rather mortgages with unsustainable characteristics that led to massive defaults at the onset of the crisis.

We also examined whether CAP loans perform well for the borrowers themselves. We find that they do: CAP households realized a return on assets better than the Dow Jones industrial average and saw a double-digit annual return on their modest equity investments. More important, most still own their homes, and their delinquency rate is well below that of both adjustable and fixed-rate subprime borrowers and even below that of adjustable-rate prime borrowers.

Has Community Reinvestment Lending Worked?

Historically homeownership has benefited middle- and higher-income Americans, who have enjoyed as a result financial gain, tenure stability, and community-level benefits. By promoting lending in low-income and minority neighborhoods, community reinvestment programs seek to broaden the opportunity to own a home. Reinvestment legislation was intended to increase access, choice, and prosperity by creating new capital where none existed, in a safe and sound manner. It was also intended to improve the lives of individual families by providing to them the benefits that homeownership engenders. Only a large-scale, in-depth investigation—an investigation the CAP data make possible for the first time—can tell us whether or not this has been the case. At long last, we are able to see what impact affordable lending has on the families that borrow through community reinvestment programs.

The CAP data allow us to examine another critical issue, too. Effective, sustainable, affordable homeownership depends on long-term investment, not speculation. Over the course of seventy years, the modern U.S. housing finance system, supported and encouraged by government experimentation and regulation, has developed the tools to make lending sound and sustainable. Through CAP, we can assess whether or not community reinvestment efforts in fact lead to sound lending.

We also investigate the results of a recent development that government policy didn't regulate, the rise of a very different source of funding for underserved borrowers. When Wall Street and the mortgage lending industry needed to find new markets and expand profitable business opportunities, these nontraditional lenders took advantage of new technologies that dramatically improved lenders' abilities to assess risks, and they fostered the development of credit scoring and risk-based pricing that led to market segmentation. They took advantage of the unmet demand that the traditional sector, despite efforts like CAP, was not serving. Regrettably, they also drove the explosive growth of the subprime mortgage market. Chapters 3 and 4 explain the very different results of subprime and community reinvestment lending.

3 | Explaining the Shadow Mortgage System

To understand the benefits of community reinvestment lending, we need to understand how it differs from another form of lending that has targeted low-income and minority communities: subprime lending. We use the term *subprime* for the industry that makes, sells, and securitizes loans that do not meet the criteria of prime, or A-grade, loans. Subprime lenders make mortgage loans to B-grade and C-grade borrowers, who are considered less likely than A-grade borrowers to repay their loans. From the get-go, lenders and investors designated subprime loans as nonconforming, which means the government-sponsored enterprises Fannie Mae and Freddie Mac could not securitize them.

As we outline in chapter 2, the mainstream mortgage market and community reinvestment lending evolved from a blend of regulation and incentives. Tax preferences, implicit government support, deposit insurance, and the full faith and credit backing of government-insured loans worked together to support public and private interests. But in recent years an alternative mortgage system developed largely outside that policy and regulatory framework. What Pimco's Paul McCulley dubs the "shadow banking system" would undermine progress in—and threaten to undo the functioning of—the U.S. mortgage market and financial markets worldwide.[1] That demise entailed both systemic failure, in the form of a catastrophic absence of necessary regulation, and product failure, in the form of unsound and predatory loans and lending practices.

We examine both aspects of this failure here. As we do so, we outline how the housing finance system is set up. By tracing the network of borrowers, brokers, lenders, ratings agencies, and secondary-market investors who had a role in the crisis, we identify what aspects of the system need regulating if another crisis is to be avoided.

Lending in the Shadows

The shadow banking system relies nearly exclusively on private funding. Because this sector did not receive any identifiable government support, lawmakers did not view it as a vehicle for advancing policy and did not consider it in need of regulation to promote safety and soundness. Instead, government leaders assumed investors would regulate themselves. Savvy investors were thought capable of managing risk, given the analytical tools available to their advisers as well as the input of the credit-rating agencies, Standard & Poor's, Moody's, and Fitch.

Because the traditional market enjoyed lower costs for borrowing and capital, it held an economic edge over the shadow banking system. However, the shadow system had an advantage too: it wasn't subject to oversight and regulation, and so it could compete and win in niches where the traditional market was not willing or allowed to compete.

For many years, most of the business of the shadow banking system was in home equity and jumbo loans. Those jumbo loans were larger than FHA, Fannie Mae, and Freddie Mac were allowed to cover. Over time, however, a new development occurred in the shadow banking system: the rise of the subprime, home purchase mortgage market. It is to the development of this sector that we now turn.

How Subprime Evolved

The subprime mortgage market arose in the 1980s to extend cash-out refinance and debt consolidation loans to borrowers with weak credit but plenty of home equity. Early in the decade, however, a series of leg-islative acts removed restrictions on certain types of loan pricing and terms, allowing activity in this market to expand; these changes were part of a sustained march toward deregulation across industries. The Depository Institutions Deregulation and Monetary Control Act of 1980 led to the gradual elimination of all federal limitations on inter-est rates payable on deposits; it also exempted first-lien mortgages from all state-level laws limiting interest rates, discount points, or finance charges. The Alternative Mortgage Transaction Parity Act of 1982 authorized all housing lenders (both federally chartered and oth-ers) to "make, purchase, and enforce alternative mortgage transac-tions" such as adjustable-rate loans, loans with balloon payments, and interest-only loans.[2]

The changes these laws put into place freed banks and mortgage lenders from state usury laws and made it easier for them to sell secu-rities in the private secondary market. In 1986 the Tax Reform Act eliminated taxpayers' ability to deduct consumer loan interest from their income tax, though they could still deduct home mortgage inter-est. As a result, homeowners began shifting debt to their homes by bor-rowing against them to fund consumption and pay off consumer debt. A subset of owners did not qualify for prime loans, even though they had plenty of equity. Originally, subprime or "home equity" lending developed to serve this niche and provide cash-out refinance and debt consolidation loans. For many borrowers, even high-cost mortgage debt was cheaper than consumer debt, particularly once taxes were considered.

Once it was legally supported, subprime lending gave institutions an alternative to prime lending. This could be useful when market con-ditions changed. For instance, when interest rates rose and prime mort-gage originations declined in 1994, nondepository and monoline finance companies (that is, those that specialize in a single type of financial business) shifted their efforts to the subprime market to main-tain volume. This growth was funded by mortgage-backed securities (also called private label or asset-backed securities).[3]

Regulatory Capture and Deregulation

If the government is to tell big business men how to run their business, then don't you see that big business men have to get closer to the government even than they are now? Don't you see that they must capture the government, in order not to be restrained too much by it? Must capture the government? They have already captured it.

—Woodrow Wilson

Government agencies charged with regulating industry are expected to promote the public interest. But occasionally regulators appear to pursue policies favorable to industries at the expense of the public. One such example is the preemption decision in 2004 by the Office of the Comptroller of the Currency (OCC) that national banks and their mortgage banking affiliates did not have to comply with rules put in place by state antipredatory lending laws.[a] This perverse phenomenon is known as regulatory capture.

Industry always has an edge on regulators: a general asymmetry exists between regulators and the regulated. Market innovation means business practice always outpaces regulation. Issues are highly complex and information is, often justly, guarded as proprietary. Regulators and the media are heavily reliant on private sources of data; for example they rely on the National Association of Realtors for information about home prices and sales and on the Mortgage Bankers Association for information about loan delinquencies.

Further, regulated industries spend considerable resources to lobby for preferred policies. According to the Center for Responsive Politics, in the ten years before the financial crash in 2008 the finance, insurance, and real estate industry sector spent $3.2 billion on lobbying and another $1.6 billion in direct campaign contributions.[b] Unfortunately, the public is often too unaware and unorganized to provide an effective counterweight to the influence of industry.

Regulatory capture can also be influenced by the "revolving door" between public agencies and businesses. Many regulators are drawn from the regulated industries, a well-known example being Treasury Secretary, and former CEO of Goldman Sachs, Henry Paulson. According to the Center for Responsive Politics and Public Citizen, nearly 1,500 former federal employees were hired by the financial sector since the beginning of 2009 to lobby Congress and federal agencies.[c]

(continued)

What were the preferred policies of the financial industry? In a word, deregulation. Policies governing the activities of financial companies were seen as inefficient and leading to suboptimal outcomes. The financial industry's ideology held that if the red tape that restricts the free market could be cut, the economy would grow. In their view, government was the problem.

Deregulation was a bipartisan cause. Clinton administration officials like Robert Rubin and Larry Summers worked to deregulate over-the-counter derivatives and credit default swaps in the Commodity Futures Modernization Act. President Clinton also signed the Gramm-Leach-Bliley Financial Services Modernization Act, which repealed the New Deal–era legislation separating commercial and investment banking. The fervor for deregulation continued into the next administration, with the removal of leverage restrictions for select financial companies and OCC preemption. The deregulatory climate also sanctioned the lax enforcement of existing regulations by agencies with responsibility for overseeing the mortgage market, including the Federal Reserve, the SEC, and the FTC.[d]

Rising homeownership rates and soaring financial profits appeared at first to justify the new regulatory paradigm. But the subsequent economic collapse, unprecedented since the Great Depression, has led some of the free market's most ardent cheerleaders to reexamine their beliefs. As former chairman of the Federal Reserve and free-market champion Alan Greenspan famously admitted, "I found a flaw . . . in the model that I perceived is the critical functioning structure that defines how the world works."[e]

The authors thank Kevin Park for his work on this and several other sidebars in the book.

a. Lei Ding and others, "The Impact of Anti-Predatory Lending Laws and Federal Preemption on Mortgage Foreclosures," report, Center for Community Capital, 2011 (www.ccc.unc.edu/abstracts/preemptionEffect.php).

b. See www.opensecrets.org/industries/indus.php?cycle=2010&ind=F.

c. See www.opensecrets.org/news/FinancialRevolvingDoors.pdf.

d. The Financial Crisis Inquiry Commission, *Final Report of the National Commission on the Causes of the Financial and Economic Crisis in the United States,* January 2011 (www.fcic.gov/report).

e. See www.pbs.org/newshour/bb/business/july-dec08/crisishearing_10-23.html.

Table 3-1. *Underwriting and Loan Grades*

Loan grade	Mortgage delinquency in days	Foreclosures	Bankruptcy, chapter 7	Bankruptcy, chapter 13	Debt ratio (%)
Premier plus (A+)	0 × 30 × 12	>36 months	Discharged >36 months	Discharged >24 months	50
Premier (A)	1 × 30 × 12	>36 months	Discharged >36 months	Discharged >24 months	50
A–	2 × 30 × 12	>36 months	Discharged >36 months	Discharged >24 months	50
B	1 × 60 × 12	>24 months	Discharged >24 months	Discharged >18 months	50
C	1 × 90 × 12	>12 months	Discharged >12 months	Filed >12 months	50
C–	2 × 90 × 12	>1 day	Discharged	Pay	50

Source: Data from Countrywide (www.csbc.com); see Souphala Chomsisengphet and Anthony Pennington-Cross, "The Evolution of the Subprime Mortgage Market," *Federal Reserve Bank of St. Louis Review* 88, no. 1 (2006): 31–56.

In this way, the B– and C-grade niches were born. At some point a new category, Alternative-A (Alt-A), was added between prime and subprime loans. Alt-A loans are considered riskier than prime loans but not as risky as B– and C-grade subprime loans. The various letter grades for loans were a product of the new computer-based rating technologies that emerged in the 1980s and 1990s. Using such factors as down payment, debt-to-income ratio, and credit history, lenders assign borrowers into categories designated by letters.

Table 3-1 lays out a rubric that Countrywide, a major subprime lender, used to determine loan grades. For this lender, a premier plus (or A+) borrower would have had no mortgage delinquencies of thirty days in the last twelve months (0 × 30 × 12), would not have experienced foreclosure or chapter 7 bankruptcy within thirty-six months, would not have experienced chapter 13 bankruptcy within twenty-four months, and would have a total debt-to-income ratio of 50 percent or less. A premier (or A-grade) borrower would have had no more than one thirty-day delinquency (1 × 30 × 12), and so on.

Loan grade does not determine the exact cost of borrowing (that is, the interest rate on the loan), which is instead determined by a borrower's credit score and loan-to-value ratio requirements. However, loan grades are used by lenders to characterize the possible risk associated with lending to different borrowers, and this presumed risk does play a part in the general pricing of a mortgage loan. Table 3-2 shows more specifically how Countrywide used different combinations of risk factors to determine the interest rate it charged on its loans.

The nonprime market—subprime and Alt-A combined—made mortgages worth $40 billion in 1990, less than 10 percent of the total mortgage market. As of the mid-1990s, the nonprime share of the market stood at 12 percent, and it would remain there through 2003.[4] The top B– and C-grade lenders included The Associates, the Money Store, Beneficial Finance, Household Financial, and Equicredit, a list that didn't overlap much with the lenders—mostly regulated depositories—at the top of the mainstream mortgage market.[5]

Fast forward to 2006. The nonprime market had become the mainstream. Its volume had grown more than tenfold over the preceding decade. Leading traditional lenders had entered the B– and C-grade market themselves. In fact many banks and thrifts got into the private market by acquiring subprime lending companies, acquisitions they often structured to minimize exposure to regulatory oversight. Unregulated affiliates could earn healthy profits without coming under the scrutiny of bank regulators.

How was the secondary market responding to this shift? By 2005 this market was issuing more private label securities than government-related securities (figure 3-1). Because private securities cannot rely upon the government-sponsored enterprises (GSEs) to protect investors from default risk, issuers found alternative and apparently cost-effective ways to price and absorb risk and to convert pools of high-risk loans into highly rated investments. Their tools included sophisticated financial models, hedges, derivatives, and complex securities structures.

Tim Geithner, then overseeing Wall Street as president of the Federal Reserve Bank of New York, saw these tools as good things. "By

Table 3-2. *Underwriting and Interest Rates*
Percent

Loan grade	Credit score	Loan-to-value ratio				
		60	70	80	90	100
Premier plus (A+)	680	5.65	5.75	5.80	5.90	7.50
	660	5.65	5.75	5.85	6.00	7.85
	600	5.75	5.80	5.90	6.60	8.40
	580	5.75	5.85	6.00	6.90	8.40
	500	6.40	6.75	7.90	...	...
Premier (A)	680	5.80	5.90	5.95	5.95	7.55
	660	5.80	5.90	6.00	6.05	7.90
	600	5.90	5.95	6.05	6.65	8.45
	580	5.90	6.00	6.15	6.95	...
	500	6.55	6.90	8.05	...	...
A–	680	...	...	...	...	...
	660	6.20	6.25	6.35	6.45	...
	600	6.35	6.45	6.50	6.70	...
	580	6.35	6.45	6.55	7.20	...
	500	6.60	6.95	8.50	...	...
B	680	...	...	...	...	...
	660	6.45	6.55	6.65	...	...
	600	6.55	6.60	6.75	...	...
	580	6.55	6.65	6.85	...	...
	500	6.75	7.25	9.20	...	...
C	680	...	...	...	...	...
	660	...	...	...	...	...
	600	6.95	7.20	...	...	...
	580	7.00	7.30	...	...	...
	500	7.45	8.95	...	...	...
C–	680	...	...	...	...	...
	660	...	...	...	...	...
	600	...	...	...	...	...
	580	7.40	7.90	...	...	...
	500	8.10	9.80	...	...	...

Source: See table 3-1.

spreading risk more broadly, providing opportunities to manage and hedge risk, and making it possible to trade and price credit risk, credit market innovation should help make markets both more efficient and more resilient," he said in 2007.[6]

Figure 3-1. *Mortgage-Backed Securities, Market Share, 1990–2007*

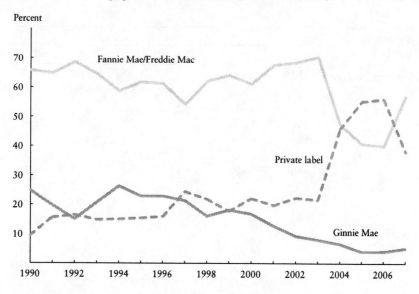

Source: *Inside Mortgage Finance, The 2009 Mortgage Market Statistical Annual.* Bethesda, Md.: Inside Mortgage Finance Publications, 2009.

In the credit market, innovation did indeed take off. The nonprime product menu expanded from fixed-rate, home equity cash-out loans to include a menu of exotic and nontraditional mortgage products. These were so complex that many borrowers and investors did not quite understand what they were getting themselves, and everyone else, into. The chair of the Federal Reserve lauded this state of affairs as the natural result of a freely functioning market. "Innovation," announced Alan Greenspan in 2005, "has brought about a multitude of new products, such as subprime loans and niche credit programs for immigrants. Such developments are representative of the market responses that have driven the financial services industry throughout the history of our country."[7]

With their market share dwindling and shareholders to appease, Fannie Mae and Freddie Mac eventually reacted to the booming subprime market by loosening their guidelines and becoming active buyers of highly rated subprime and Alt-A loans and securities.

Financial Instruments with a Role in the Economic Crisis

Collateralized debt obligation (CDO): A pool of debt instruments (like bonds) where the revenue stream is divided into shares. Typically these shares, or tranches, are given different levels of priority in case of default in the underlying pool of assets, leading to different levels of risk and return for each tranche. During the mortgage-backed security boom, investors received higher returns for the so-called equity tranche, which held the riskiest investments.

Credit default swap (CDS): A financial instrument that acts like an insurance policy on a particular bond or security. In exchange for a fee, one company agrees to compensate another company for losses in a particular investment. Banks and other companies that issue credit default swaps earn fees for insuring events they think highly unlikely. The company issuing the CDS is required to post collateral to cover the swap, but in general this collateral is not sufficient to provide true coverage. This means that the credit default swap market is undercapitalized, a situation that had drastic financial repercussions when the mortgage-backed security market collapsed and the companies that issued credit default swaps were unprepared to cover the resulting losses.[a]

Derivative: A tradable security in which nothing tangible is actually exchanged but whose value is derived from the actual or expected price of some underlying asset. The most common types of derivatives are futures, options, and swaps. In a futures contract, two parties agree to exchange an asset in the future for a price agreed upon today. In an options contract, one party obtains the right to buy or sell an asset in the future for a price agreed upon today, but the party is not required to complete the transaction. In a swap, parties agree to exchange investment assets or cash flows at specified times in the future.

Hedge: An attempt to reduce financial risk by undertaking offsetting financial activities. For example, if a business has to hold stocks of a commodity, it risks losses if the price falls. Losses can be avoided, however, if the business hedges by selling the good forward—that is, for delivery at an agreed price on a future date.[b]

(continued)

Mortgage-backed security (MBS): A security made up of the income stream from a pool of mortgages. A security is a financial instrument that takes advantage of safety in numbers: a security allows you to own, instead of a single asset, an equivalent share in a pool of assets. In an MBS, you might own a 1 percent stake in a hundred different mortgages. If ten borrowers in the underlying pool default, this merely reduces your income stream, rather than cutting it off completely.

a. "Times Topics: Credit Default Swaps," *New York Times*, May 21, 2010 (http://topics.nytimes.com/top/reference/timestopics/subjects/c/credit_default_sw aps/index.html?pagewanted=all).

b. John Black, *A Dictionary of Economics* (Oxford University Press, 1997).

Heading for a Meltdown

Fannie Mae and Freddie Mac have traditionally held significant assets on their books, primarily in the form of mortgage-backed securities that they themselves issued. By the mid-2000s, however, their purchases of private label mortgage-backed securities had increased dramatically, rising from $28 billion in 2001 to $221 billion in 2005.[8] To their credit, the GSEs claimed they wanted to bring discipline to the market and so refused to buy securities backed by loans with particularly predatory features. They also restricted their purchases to the highest rated portions of subprime and Alt-A securities.

Though they bought these mortgage-backed securities mainly for reasons of profit and market share, the GSEs were allowed to count the underlying loans toward their affordable housing goals providing the loans met the specified criteria. Through these purchases, the GSEs added hundreds of billions of dollars to the already overheated private market and encouraged a fundamental shift from the public to the private sector and, essentially, from the promotion of public goals to the pursuit of private gains.

By 2006 the mortgage market was disintegrating into chaos. Subprime foreclosures were mounting. May 2006 saw the first lender col-

Exotic Mortgage Products

Hybrid adjustable-rate mortgages: Mortgages that involve an initial period (usually two to five years), during which the mortgage's interest rate is fixed at a relatively low level, after which the interest rate can adjust as often as every six months. Because the initial fixed rate is sometimes artificially low, borrowers may be caught off guard when the rate resets and they are unable to meet the higher monthly payments.

Interest-only mortgage: A mortgage in which only the interest on the principal is paid for a set amount of time. (A traditional mortgage is self-amortizing, meaning monthly payments pay down both interest and the remaining principal of the loan.) The interest-only payment period is typically between three and ten years, after which the monthly payments increase (even if the interest rate is fixed), because the borrower must begin repaying the principal as well as the interest.

Option adjustable-rate mortgage: A mortgage that allows a variety of payment options every month, ranging from paying both interest and principal (which reduces principal), to paying only interest (which leaves principal level), to paying a minimum amount that does not even cover the monthly interest (which increases principal). The latter constitutes negative amortization, where the unpaid interest is added to the principal of the mortgage, increasing the indebtedness of the borrower.

lapse of the crisis. By March 2007 the private secondary market started to crumble. In January 2008, Countrywide Financial, the top lender from 2004 through 2007, was subsumed into Bank of America. September 2008 would see the government taking Fannie Mae and Freddie Mac into conservatorship in order to keep the market functioning. Overexposed to subprime securities, Lehman Brothers Holdings failed in the middle of that month, rocking the money markets. Days later, to head off global financial panic, the federal government would bail out American Insurance Group (AIG) and announce the $700 billion Troubled Asset Relief Program (TARP). Ripple effects throughout the economy would drag home prices down 30 percent and drive unemployment up to 10 percent by the end of 2009.

What led the market to alter so drastically by 2006? Several long-term trends—the segmentation enabled by automated underwriting and risk-based pricing, an excess of capital fueling an overheated private secondary market, a gross misallocation of risk, a lack of regulation, and a house price bubble—all converged to dramatically alter the mortgage landscape in a few short years. In a short time, this hazardous combination undermined the homeownership gains of the preceding decades. We examine each of these factors in turn.

The Rise of Risk-Based Lending

In the traditional mortgage market, everyone who qualifies for a loan gets more or less the same product for the same price. Lenders expand access to housing finance by incrementally adjusting their lending requirements and blending the risk of new entrants into the risk of the entire pool. For instance, to meet their affordable housing goals Fannie Mae and Freddie Mac were directed to encourage lenders to develop "prudent and appropriate underwriting standards," taking into account the circumstances of low- and moderate-income families. To achieve this goal, lenders might accept evidence of consistent and timely bill payment for borrowers without an established credit score; they also might allow borrowers to use monetary gifts from family and friends toward their down payments or encourage homeownership counseling for applicants who were less financially secure.

Instead of expanding access to a standard mortgage product, risk-based lending opened multiple new lending paths, each with its own prices and terms. This shift occurred as lenders began to qualify borrowers by relying on credit scores rather than on detailed credit reports. Credit scoring models have been around since the 1950s, when retail stores and finance companies began to use their own internal data to make decisions about extending credit to their customers.[9]

In the 1980s technological advances made it possible for credit bureaus to track a given borrower's payment history with multiple lenders. Experian, Equifax, and TransUnion, the three major credit bureaus, aggregate the payment information they collect. Fair Isaac calculates a FICO score using information from the three bureaus. The score reflects the likelihood that a given borrower will become seriously delinquent on any open credit account in the next eighteen to twenty-four months.[10] Lending institutions began relying on credit scores to develop, market, and underwrite products. These new technologies allowed lenders to rank borrowers by risk, and in this way the use of credit scores became intertwined with the rise of risk-based loan pricing. By 2000 almost every mortgage loan decision depended in part on the borrower's credit score.[11]

For borrowers who were previously shut out of the mainstream mortgage market or were on its margins, lenders developed relaxed underwriting requirements tailored to match their estimation of borrowers' risk levels. In exchange, these borrowers paid more for their loans or obtained loans at increased costs. In addition to higher interest rates, borrowers might have to pay higher upfront fees, lock themselves into a loan with a prepayment penalty, agree to pay off the loan in a lump sum (balloon payment) after several years, or use some form of adjustable-rate loan. The problem is that these higher cost features, seemingly tailored to reflect borrower risk, actually increased mortgage costs to the point where the loan itself made the risk of default more likely.

These higher cost, higher risk options dramatically expanded access to credit, and Alan Greenspan, for one, approved. In 2005 he said, "Lenders have taken advantage of credit-scoring models and other techniques for efficiently extending credit to a broader spectrum of consumers. . . . Where once more-marginal applicants would simply have been denied credit, lenders are now able to quite efficiently judge the risk posed by individual applicants and to price that risk appropriately. These improvements have led to rapid growth in subprime mortgage lending."[12]

However, few would now extol subprime lending's most egregious form: predatory lending. Predatory lending is identified by a list of unfair and abusive practices that destroy homeowner wealth: excessive

How Predatory Lending Strips Homeowner Equity

Accounts from the media, bankruptcy courts, and credit counseling agencies around the country provide the basis for this typical predatory lending story. Mary Smith has built up substantial equity by paying down a thirty-year, fixed-rate mortgage on a modest home whose value has appreciated. Her house needs minor repairs, as is apparent from the exterior, but she has put off making them because she is on a fixed income. A mortgage broker approaches her and offers a new loan to pay off the small balance on her existing mortgage and extract a little equity to fix the front entranceway. The broker tells Mary it won't cost her anything out of pocket, and she trusts him and agrees. They set a closing date, and the broker tells her she can stop making payments on her old mortgage.

At closing, the new loan amount includes thousands of dollars' worth of fees designated for the broker and other parties, of whom Mary was previously unaware. The interest rate is also higher than Mary remembers agreeing to; what she doesn't know is that the lending company will increase the broker's fee if Mary agrees to the loan's higher interest rate.

When Mary raises her concerns, the broker reminds her that she is already two months behind on her existing mortgage. With such a blemish on her credit, he says, she won't be able to borrow from anyone else at this point. He also points out that her payments are actually going down because the new loan, while larger than the balance of the old loan, is amortized over a much longer period.

A few months after closing, the broker calls on Mary again and points out that the loan has a balloon payment, meaning she must pay it off in full in five years. This worries Mary, so the broker offers to make her a new loan without this balloon feature. Once again, the loan is packed with fees, including enough to pay off the 3 percent prepayment penalty of the prior loan.

This process will repeat: whenever the increasing burden gets too much, Mary can get a larger loan and buy a little time. By switching to an adjustable rate, she can temporarily lower her payments, but they will only skyrocket later. Unless Mary can find a way to refinance to a safer loan before the indebtedness gets out of control, foreclosure is almost inevitable.

What prevents Mary from refinancing back to a lower cost, safer mortgage? For one thing, prepayment penalties make it costly to refinance. Moreover, the lending company has not reported appropriately to the credit bureaus, so Mary's payment history appears worse than it actually is. Furthermore, when Mary tries to find out how to refinance and how much she actually owes, the lending company gives her the runaround.

Many of the victims of practices such as these were long-term homeowners, many elderly or disabled. All lost at least a portion of their home equity through outsized fees, and many lost their homes entirely through foreclosure. The Center for Responsible Lending estimated in 2001 that the cost of interest rate overcharges and home equity stripped away by finance fees was over $9 billion annually.[a]

a. Center for Responsible Lending, "Predatory Lending Annual Toll is $9.1 Billion," 2001 (www.responsiblelending.org/media-center/press-releases/archives/predatory-lending-annual-toll-is-9-1-billion.html), report to be released to U.S. Senate.

fees and hidden penalties, broker kickbacks, repeated flipping to impose additional fees, mandatory arbitration clauses that limit borrowers' legal rights, bait and switch terms, and unethical loan-servicing practices.

Excess Capital and the Insatiable Demand for Mortgage-Backed Securities

The late 1990s marked the start of a period of oversupply of capital around the globe. In 2005, pension, insurance, and mutual funds around the world had $46 trillion at their disposal, up almost a third from 2000.[13] Investors needed somewhere to put this excess capital, and they were looking for profits. With its promise of higher yields, the growing market in securities backed by subprime mortgages attracted investors from around the world.

In an effort to meet the seemingly insatiable demand for mortgage-backed securities, lenders loosened their underwriting standards so that they could originate more mortgages, which could then be sold for packaging into securities. Down payments got smaller, and lenders paid less and less attention to borrowers' ability to repay. Documentation of income and assets relaxed, and eventually lenders didn't require any evidence at all—they simply asked applicants to state what their income and assets were. These "stated income" and "stated asset" loans, designed for creditworthy, self-employed borrowers who could not easily produce W-2 forms, became widespread among regular wage earners.

Each innovation opened new opportunities to produce more loans. Those who earned fees for originating mortgages had a financial incentive to issue as many as possible. Originators of subprime mortgages got paid up front by borrowers (who often financed the fees through the loan amount) and by lenders. Then they passed the loans to the lenders and were out of the picture, profiting even if borrowers later defaulted. Lenders in turn sold the loans to Wall Street, who packaged them into increasingly complex securities.[14] Credit-rating agencies, which were paid by the Wall Street firms that issued these investments, rated the securities as solid. The firms then sold these "solid" securities to investors.

As the fervor built, enormous amounts of capital from all around the world flowed to the private mortgage securities market. Investors were drawn by the allure of high yields and were reassured by the high ratings on these securities. The market's growing appetite for private label mortgage-backed securities increased the flow of capital to nonprime and unregulated lenders. These lenders captured market share from those areas of the traditional, regulated channel where risk and capital rules still held sway. The old, traditional channel between capital markets and borrowers—Fannie Mae and Freddie Mac—began to look like unnecessary friction with added costs and underwriting requirements. The GSEs became increasingly marginal. In 2004 alone, Fannie Mae and Freddie Mac's business fell by more than half.

Gross Miscalculation of Risk

Without governmental or quasi-governmental guarantors, those who issued private market securities have to find alternative ways to distribute the risk associated with these investments. One way to do this was through the issuance of collateralized debt obligations (CDOs) composed of mortgage-backed securities.

CDOs were so complex, however, that the ratings agencies failed to accurately assess the risk associated with them. A 2008 Securities and Exchange Commission (SEC) investigation finds that the ratings agencies it examined lacked adequate rating procedures. Furthermore, the agencies didn't always disclose or even document significant aspects of the rating process. Finally, "conflicts of interest were not always managed appropriately"—that is, those issuing the ratings had a stake in making the investments look less risky than they in fact were.[15]

When subprime mortgages began defaulting en masse, the CDO market collapsed and investors called in their bets. Bond insurers who had become heavily involved in guaranteeing highly rated tranches of CDOs were downgraded, and some failed entirely, creating a ripple effect on state and local government borrowing. The failure of Lehman Brothers Holdings—a major holder of credit default swaps (CDSs)—almost triggered a run on money market funds. AIG's huge, worldwide CDS liability prompted a bailout by the U.S. government to avert a financial domino effect.[16]

The complex financial engineering process that appeared to dissipate the risk associated with increasingly slipshod lending in fact only served to mask it. As a result, many participants were exposed to a level of risk that they did not recognize, had not charged for, and did not hold capital against. The U.S. taxpayer had to step in to prevent a total collapse of the financial system.

Fiddling While Rome Burned

Where were the regulators who should have kept all of this risky behavior in check? Instead of reining in the rampant and risky sub-

How Risk Is Distributed in Private Label Securitization

Ginnie Mae, Fannie Mae, and Freddie Mac guarantee repayment of the securities they issue. By contrast, the private sector had to find other ways to distribute the risk inherent in its mortgage-backed securities. Here we explain how they did it.

Imagine a hundred mortgages. Each individual loan will either default or pay, but issuers can't predict which ones will do which. Putting them together in a pool allows them to make a reasonably good prediction of how much money they will lose and how much they will be paid, across all hundred loans. Then they can sell interests in this pool in the form of mortgage-backed securities (MBSs). Some investors want more risk and return, while others want a safe investment with no losses. So those packaging the securities divide the flow of monthly payments into tranches, which are paid in a different order to different investors. Investors with the greatest risk appetite buy the subordinated tranches and will get paid whatever is left after all other investors get paid. If enough borrowers stop paying, these lowest tranches get nothing, and the next lowest tranche might stop paying dividends, and so on. The top tranches—usually the bulk of the investments—are rated AAA or AA. The very bottom tranche, the equity tranche, will be unrated and might be impossible to sell.

What can the private sector do with these higher risk tranches that are tying up capital? They can go one step further and bundle several of these in a pool. Then they divide this pool of risky investments into tranches and sell them as collateralized debt obligations (CDOs). Now, even though the underlying tranches were all high risk, the CDO gives the appearance of having lower risk segments. In this way CDO issuers managed to sell off their riskier investments, reducing the capital they had to hold against the initial MBS transaction.

Think of a pool of loans as a glass of pond water, with particles (representing risk) that cloud the water, even though it's impossible to see each individual particle. No one wants to drink that. As the glass sits, however, the dirt settles, with the heaviest sludge at the bottom and the cleanest water at the top (like tranches). The clear water could be drunk. If the clear water from a number of glasses was drunk and the sludgy residue from all the glasses were combined, eventually it will separate further, at least somewhat. But would it be safe to drink the water at the top of that bottle?

The final bottle of sludge is like a CDO. The ratings agencies gave good ratings to many such investments; as many as 80 percent of CDOs got AAA ratings, even though they were largely composed of risky elements.[a] Meanwhile, evaluating the risk of these investments got infinitely more complex than evaluating the risk of the initial underlying assets (the original hundred loans).

One astonishing development during the subprime lending debacle was the creation of the credit default swap (CDS). If market participants didn't want to bear the risks associated with their CDOs, they could get someone else to cover their bets by using a CDS. Under this mechanism, one company would pay a fee to another company (say AIG or Lehman, which were major issuers of CDSs) in exchange for their agreement to pay any future losses on that investment. There could be multiple CDSs on the same risk, which made the total CDS market several times larger than the value of the underlying assets. In 2008 the Securities Industry and Financial Market Association estimated that the sum of all forms of asset-backed debt in the United States was about $10 trillion, while the sum of all CDSs was about $55 trillion.[b]

Is it any wonder, given this scenario, that when subprime mortgages started to default in large numbers, this set off a chain reaction that nearly caused a global financial meltdown?

a. Kathleen C. Engel and Patricia A. McCoy, *The Subprime Virus* (Oxford University Press, 2011).

b. "The $55 Trillion Question," CNNMoney, 2008 (http://money.cnn.com/ 2008/09/30/magazines/fortune/varchaver_derivatives_short.fortune/index.htm? postversion=2008093012).

prime market, regulators provided strong market signals for reckless lending to continue unabated. Their actions encouraged the provision of easy credit and nontraditional mortgages. They also manifested a laissez-faire attitude by failing to take regulatory action.

Economists believe that the Federal Reserve's decision in mid-2003 to reduce the federal funds rate to 1 percent and to hold it low for a year was an important factor in the ensuing crisis. The Fed cut the rate in response to deflation fears. Keeping interest rates low encouraged the borrowing that led to higher prices. Consequently, mortgage lending was one of the few growth industries in the United States.

At the same time, the Fed was encouraging Americans to assume more risk in their borrowing behavior. In a 2004 speech, Alan Greenspan even encouraged borrowers to choose adjustable-rate mortgages: "American consumers might benefit if lenders provided greater mortgage product alternatives to the traditional fixed-rate mortgage. To the degree that households are driven by fears of payment shocks but are willing to manage their own interest rate risks, the traditional fixed-rate mortgage may be an expensive method of financing a home."[17] With such encouragement, it is not surprising that lenders began to offer ever more exotic products, regardless of their appropriateness to the circumstances of individual borrowers.

To try to clamp down on reckless lending, states began passing their own mortgage-lending laws, something North Carolina had been the first to do in 1999. Consumer advocates and affordable housing advocates called for Congress to take action and for the Federal Reserve to use the powers granted to it to provide consumer protection at the national level. But Washington seemed uninterested in reining in the banking industry. Quite the opposite: federal regulators actually exempted national lenders and their subsidiaries from state laws aimed at curtailing the worst lending practices.

Why this lack of intervention? We suggest three reasons. The first was ideological. The Bush administration and then Federal Reserve Chairman Greenspan shared a belief that markets police themselves effectively. Market discipline should result when it is in the best interest of market participants to monitor the risks that those they do business with take on. When stakeholders have incentives to keep tabs on these risks, counterparties who engage in irresponsible practices are weaned out of the market. In theory, this discipline corrects market inefficiencies and prevents failures. Unfortunately, this theory has proven fallible.[18]

The second reason for government inaction may have been more pragmatic. Consumer spending accounts for over two-thirds of all economic activity in the United States. Between 2000 and 2005, wages remained relatively flat. Those with the lowest incomes saw their real earnings increase by only 3 percent during the 1990s.[19] As incomes failed to keep pace with living costs and consumption, borrowing against home equity grew. Thus as home prices continued to rise during the 1990s and 2000s, consumption was facilitated in large part by a reliance on home equity. In 2003 about half of all subprime loans (810,000) served to refinance existing mortgages. Of these subprime refinances, about 560,000 (70 percent) were cash-out refinances.[20] This additional cash allowed families to maintain or increase consumption despite minimal earnings growth. The administration in power probably did not want to curtail economic activity by limiting the availability of loans, however untenable, that made possible consumption and economic growth—and the optimism attending both.

The third reason policymakers failed to act was political. Together, the finance, insurance, and real estate (FIRE) sectors hold significant sway on Capitol Hill, leading all other sectors in lobbying expenditures for the decade ending in 2007. Between 1998 and 2006, when the crisis began, FIRE lobbying expenditures increased from about $200 million to almost $400 million. Similarly, FIRE campaign contributions increased significantly during the 2000s, to peak at almost $500 million in 2008. The sector is the largest source of campaign contributions to federal candidates and political parties, with insurance companies, securities and investment firms, real estate interests, and commercial banks providing the bulk of that money. Members of the FIRE sector contribute generously to Republicans and Democrats alike. For example, the sector gave at least 55 percent of their contributions to the GOP between 1996 to 2004. Not surprisingly, starting in 2008, FIRE has made higher donations to the Democrats, who at the time con-

Figure 3-2. *Homeownership, Price-to-Income Ratio, 1990–2009*

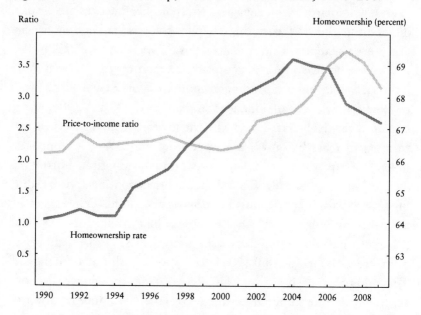

Source: U.S. Census Bureau, *Housing Vacancy Survey, Current Population Survey.*

trolled the White House and Congress.[21] A politician who clamped down on the mortgage market bonanza during the rapid subprime expansion would have been committing political suicide.

House Price Inflation and Risk-Free Buying

Even as incomes stagnated, U.S. house prices continued to climb. Price increases were fueled by low interest rates, excess capital, and the underpricing of risk. Figure 3-2 shows that the ratio of house price to income remained steady before 2000, suggesting that the homeownership gains from 1994 into the early 2000s were sustainable. But in the early 2000s, house price increases far outpaced income growth even as homeownership rates continued to climb. At its peak, the median home price was nearly five times the median income.

How could this happen? Economics 101 teaches that as prices rise, demand should fall. But as interest rates fall, the monthly payment for the same size mortgage falls too. When prime mortgage rates hit a peak of 8 percent in 2000, the payment on a $250,000 mortgage was about $1,835. When those rates fell to 5.5 percent in 2004, the payment shrank to about $1,420. The person who could qualify for a $250,000 loan in 2000 could afford the payments on a $330,000 loan in 2004. Lower rates enable people to pay more for a house, and when people can pay more, prices tend to rise.

A long period of rising home values led to the expectation that buying a house was a sure thing. Because property values would continue to rise, they would offset borrower risk—or so the thinking went. As more borrowers qualified for larger mortgages, demand rose, which further fed home prices. Appreciation fueled easy credit, which in turn fueled more appreciation. As home prices accelerated, speculators entered the market. So did ordinary people who feared they would miss their last chance to purchase a home.

To facilitate easier access to credit, lenders designed riskier, adjustable-rate mortgages, many of which had a low introductory or teaser rate. They promoted these subprime and Alt-A loans on the premise that, with increases in house values, families could easily refinance or sell when their payments got too big. How did these riskier mortgages relate to house prices? Each "innovation" in lending allowed potential homebuyers to bid more for housing, feeding the price bubble (figure 3-3). We identify the markets where credit was easiest to obtain and those where house prices rose the most during the bubble years. The states where subprime lending had the highest share of the market experienced the highest rates of house price appreciation during the bubble years. These same markets saw house prices tumble the farthest after 2007 (figure 3-4).

Acting Rationally

The dynamics at play as house prices rose go beyond "irrational exuberance," to use Greenspan's term for unwarranted market optimism. Those who participated in the housing market responded rationally to economic incentives, as can be seen in the following theoretical example.

Figure 3-3. *House Price Change, by State Subprime Share, 2001–06*

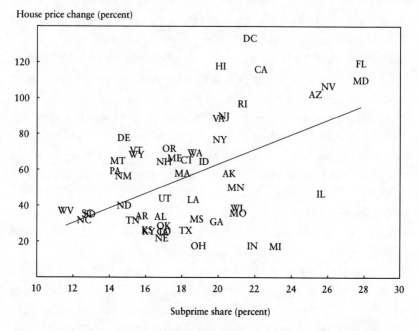

House price change (percent)

Source: Roberto G. Quercia and Lei Ding, "Tailoring Loan Modifications: When Is Principle Reduction Desirable?" (Center for Community Capital, University of North Carolina, 2009).

Jill and Jack are identical from an underwriting perspective, with the same income, assets, credit scores, and employment histories. But they have very different attitudes about risk. They are both trying to buy George's house, and each can make a monthly payment of around $1,000. Being more risk averse, Jill prequalifies for a thirty-year, 6 percent, fixed-rate mortgage and escrow of property taxes and insurance. She should be able to borrow $160,000. In contrast, Jack prequalifies for a $250,000 adjustable-rate mortgage with a 3 percent teaser rate and no monthly escrow payments for taxes and insurance. Even if Jill makes a 20 percent down payment with her own money, she can only offer $200,000, not even close to what Jack can offer, even though he makes no down payment. It is not difficult to guess who is going to make the higher bid for George's house. George sells the house to Jack for $225,000.

Figure 3-4. *House Price Change, 2006–08, by State Subprime Share, 2001–06*

House price change (percent)

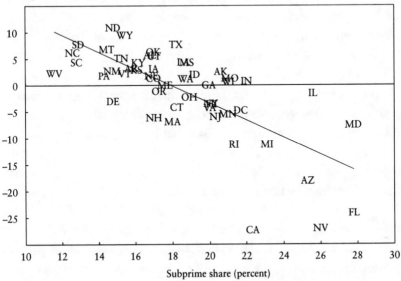

Source: See figure 3-3.

Now Maria, George's neighbor, decides to sell her house. Her real estate agent checks the recent sales in her neighborhood (including George's) and suggests that Maria set her price at $230,000, which she does. Jill is still looking for a house. She can rely again on a fixed-rate mortgage instead of a riskier product. But will her bid be successful? Not likely. Alternatively, she could try to buy a home in another neighborhood where property values are lower. For one individual, such an option may be feasible, but over time, for hundreds or thousands of Jills, the only way to buy a home in a given market will be to rely on a risky mortgage.

In this scenario, Jill's real estate agent, who encourages people to buy only as much house as they can well afford, earns lower commissions and ultimately loses business to Jack's agent, who promotes higher priced homes. Jill's mortgage broker, who counsels against taking out a risky mortgage that is only temporarily affordable, will never receive a referral from Jack's real estate agent. Likewise, the appraiser Jill's broker prefers, who carefully calculates a reasonable value regardless of whether the value justifies the offer price, will get no business from Jack's popular mortgage broker. Such impacts ripple through the home-buying process all the way to the agencies that rate pools of loans for the secondary market. A ratings agency will not be hired to rate the next deal if it is too tough on the pool that holds Jack's loan.

As our example shows, market participants responding rationally to a range of short-term economic incentives became caught up in a self-reinforcing cycle. Concerned about deflation, the government and the regulators reduced the cost of credit and promoted nontraditional mortgage instruments. That drove up prices. Investors' and lenders' demand for high-yielding investments led them to create and promote ever more innovative mortgage products, which allowed loan applicants to borrow more money with fewer requirements and restrictions. With each lending innovation, home purchasers bid the price of houses up ever higher. Ironically, advocates for affordable housing and fair lending, who once pushed so hard for increased access to housing finance for underserved populations, now found themselves calling for restraint in lending practices. Unfortunately, lawmakers and regulators ignored them.

What Triggered the Crisis?

Given the state of the housing finance market in late 2006 and early 2007, it is little wonder that a collapse ensued. Rising nonprime defaults caused a crisis of confidence. When ratings agencies finally took a careful hard look at nonprime mortgage assets, they started downgrading securities. As the value of subprime assets tumbled, institutional capital, which was razor thin to begin with at many firms, fell to critical levels.

Financial firms had no choice but to try to sell assets to raise capital and reduce debt, a process called deleveraging. But asset values fell faster than institutions could recapitalize, which caused a downward spiral. Suddenly, the global supply of capital supporting the U.S. mortgage market dried up, and property values started to fall. Bond insurers, municipal bondholders, money market funds, international investors, pension funds, and others all felt the repercussions, which continue to play out across the U.S. and global economies. The dramatic failure and rescue of the financial system caused significant and long-lasting damage to the financial security of families throughout the country. Perversely, these burdens have fallen disproportionately on low-income and minority communities and households.

Unequal Impact

As we note earlier, the market's demise was precipitated in large part by product failure, which itself resulted from regulatory failure. Our research and the work of others confirm that low-income and minority families were disproportionately offered risky, high-cost mortgages and were more likely to be subject to predatory practices. As a result, they are now suffering a higher risk of foreclosure.

Under the Home Mortgage Disclosure Act (HMDA), information about loan origination, borrower characteristics, and geographic information is compiled to reveal lending patterns. These data show that, from 2004 through 2006, about half of the mortgage loans made nationwide to African Americans and 37 percent of those made to Hispanic borrowers were high cost, compared with only 15 percent of the loans made to white families. High-income African Americans were even more likely than low-income white borrowers to receive a nonprime loan.

This is not to say that most subprime loans went to minorities. Most high-cost mortgages (52 percent) went to white borrowers. Similarly, most high-cost loans (68 percent) went not to low-income borrowers but to those making more than 80 percent of area median income. Still, minorities and low-income households received more than their proportional share of high-cost mortgages. So too did neighborhoods with higher concentrations of minority or low-income residents.

The city of Atlanta provides a case in point. We analyzed higher priced lending in that city, using the HMDA definition of higher priced (specifically, those loans in which the annual percentage rate spread is at least three percentage points higher than the yield on treasury securities of comparable maturity). We looked at all conventional first mortgages made in 2004 for owner occupants of one-to-four unit homes and added census 2000 data on neighborhood characteristics. Not surprisingly, minority borrowers and neighborhoods with greater shares of minority residents had substantially higher concentrations of high-cost lending than others. Of course, some of this might be attributable to different risk factors of borrowers or neighborhoods. So we set out to see if, after taking those risk factors into account, these disparities still held. We considered a number of variables for each census tract: median income level, how many properties were investment properties, housing turnover rates, the denial rates for conventional loan applications (a proxy for credit risk), and median house age.

Even after controlling for these factors, the percent of mortgages that were higher cost was still significantly higher in neighborhoods with greater concentrations of African American residents. Furthermore, all else being equal, the lower the income level for households in the neighborhood, the higher the share of subprime loans. At the loan level, African American borrowers were much more likely to obtain a high-priced loan than whites were (more than three times as likely with a purchase loan and twice as likely with a refinance). Hispanic borrowers were also more likely than whites to obtain a high-priced mortgage, though not as likely as African Americans. Not surprisingly, the lower a household's income, the more likely it was to get a high-priced loan.[22]

A new question preoccupied us: How does it affect a neighborhood when many of its homeowners have subprime loans? This is an area where little research has been done, and we wondered whether the clustering of subprime loans might affect how other loans in the neighborhood perform. Only a few researchers have investigated how neighborhood characteristics affect home loan performance, and they did not consider the impact of neighborhood subprime lending.[23] We set out to fill this gap.

Using HMDA data along with information from nearly 7,000 Community Advantage Program loans, we examined how prime mortgages performed in neighborhoods with different concentrations of subprime loans. We chose to look at loans originated during the years 2004–06; this allowed us to observe the performance of affordable loans in a softening housing market. Because we utilized a very rich data set, which includes borrower and loan information, complete monthly payment history for each individual loan, and neighborhood information, we could distinguish the impact of neighborhood subprime activities from underwriting criteria and borrower characteristics.

Using these fine-grained data, we analyzed how the spatial concentration of subprime lending affects the performance of a sample of recently originated affordable mortgages. Numerous factors other than subprime lending may influence how residential mortgages perform, and we controlled for many of these, including the level of home equity, the relationship between the present discounted value of the current mortgage compared with the present discounted value of a prevailing market-rate mortgage, the borrower's credit history, loan size, loan age, borrower race, borrower income, racial and ethnic composition of the census tract, census tract median income relative to area median income, year of origination, and the monthly state unemployment rate.

We find that the concentration of subprime lending in certain neighborhoods appears to have negative effects. As the share of subprime purchase loans increased, so did the risk of default, even though the borrowers themselves did not hold subprime loans. For example, for a white borrower holding a prime mortgage originated in 2005, the probability of default and foreclosure increases with the share of subprime purchase loans in the tract where the property is located. If the borrower lives in a tract with the national average share of subprime purchase loans (25 percent), the predicted probability of default is 0.033 percent. But if he or she lives in a tract where 50 percent of the homeowners have subprime purchase loans, the predicted probability of default is 0.043 percent, some 30 percent higher.[24]

Our work reveals that the level of subprime purchase lending in a census tract is a significant predictor of the performance of prime loan products serving low- to moderate-income borrowers in these neighborhoods. A higher level of subprime purchase lending in a neighborhood increases the probability of delinquency and lowers the probability of prepayment for borrowers holding affordable loans.

Subprime mortgages are in and of themselves more likely to default. There are several reasons for this. High-cost loans have higher interest rates, which makes the monthly payments harder to carry. The inclusion of large up-front fees in the loan amount reduces equity, and borrowers with less equity are more likely to default on their loans. Then there are prepayment penalties, which trap borrowers in expensive loans; these penalties are virtually nonexistent on prime loans but have been tacked onto as many as 80 percent of nonprime mortgages. Exacerbating default risk, many nonprime loans didn't require escrow accounts to cover insurance and tax payments, leading to payment shock when these were due. Variable payment plans with adjustable rates, interest-only periods, and negative amortization all leave the borrower vulnerable to payment shock; nonprime mortgages are much more likely than prime mortgages to feature such risky elements.

Nonprime mortgages are also more likely to be originated by brokers. Researchers find that mortgages originated by brokers default at significantly higher rates than other, similar loans.[25] Brokers are not inherently wayward, but their compensation system has rewarded them for volume and for maximizing the interest rate and fees they can get the borrower to agree to. Perhaps the most disturbing aspect of the subprime lending saga is that many borrowers ended up in costlier and riskier loans than they were in fact eligible for. Lending agents all too often steered borrowers into expensive products. In 2000 Freddie Mac estimated that between 10 and 35 percent of subprime borrowers met the requirements for lower cost loans. Fannie Mae estimated that 50 percent of borrowers in the subprime market could have qualified for a prime loan.[26]

Why would people who could qualify for low-cost prime loans take out subprime mortgages? In a well-functioning, transparent market, such inefficiencies should not persist. When borrowers compare standard, traditional thirty-year, fixed-rate mortgages with no prepayment penalties or balloons, they find the task relatively easy. They simply check the newspaper, search online, or make a few phone calls. But obtaining a mortgage in the nontraditional part of the market, with its bewildering menu of products, pricing, and terms, can easily confuse borrowers, and especially those with less knowledge about the lending process. When researchers compare prime and subprime borrowers, they find that subprime borrowers are less knowledgeable about the mortgage process, less likely to search for the best rates, and less likely to be offered a choice between different types of mortgages.[27] The less the borrower understands the transaction, the more he puts himself at the mercy of the lending agent, whom he likely assumes is working on his behalf.

Why would lenders support deceptive practices that ultimately increased the risk of foreclosure? After all, brokers are paid by, and sell their loans to, other, larger entities. Some of these entities are independent mortgage companies; many are banks or bank owned. In fact, many banks and thrifts were making good profits in the nonprime business, directly, through affiliates, and through capital markets operations. With one hand, these institutions rationed the supply of low-cost, safe mortgages while, with the other, they dispensed a risky, untenable substitute. The excesses in nonprime lending led to a financial crisis that affected everyone. But it is the very communities that had long been denied equal access to housing finance that were disproportionately targeted with the riskiest loans. These families are bearing the brunt of foreclosures, ruined credit, and lost homes. It is a cruel irony that those families and neighborhoods that once found it hard to get access to credit now find themselves with an oversupply of toxic loans.

Throughout this tumultuous period in U.S. mortgage markets, though, thousands of lower income and minority borrowers navigated a safe way into homeownership. They were served by housing counselors, down payment assistance programs, and reasonable approaches to flexible underwriting. Anecdotally, localities report that programs that incorporate such efforts experience lower defaults, even in these turbulent times. We set out to examine one such program in depth in order to distinguish once and for all how affordable lending can be undertaken safely and sustainably. Our findings form the basis of the next chapter.

4 | *Lending for the Long Term*

Community reinvestment lending and subprime lending have some similarities. Both make mortgages available to families that previously had limited access to credit typically because of insufficient income or low credit scores; lower income and minority households in particular benefited from Community Reinvestment Act (CRA) lending. Our research shows, however, that the two kinds of lending have very different outcomes. Community reinvestment mortgages, such as those in the Community Advantage Program (CAP), have significantly lower rates of default than subprime loans. The big question is why; what accounts for the sharp differences in the results of subprime and community reinvestment lending?

To answer this question, we looked in depth at evidence from the loans within the CAP portfolio. At the Center for Community Capital (CCC) we have been tracking over 46,000 affordable home loans since origination, and we have been speaking annually for each of the past six years with over 2,000 of these homeowners. Our research gives us an insider's view of how lower income homeowners benefit from community reinvestment lending. While the mortgage market melted down and the foreclosure rate for subprime borrowers skyrocketed, we watched families that participate in CAP enjoy continued homeownership and sustained, if moderate, wealth gains. How was this possible?

The answer lies in part in the starkly different goals of the two types of business. In a way, the two types of lending are flip sides of the same coin, both focused on providing housing finance to borrowers who do not have ready access to credit. However, community reinvestment lending aims to foster long-term homeownership, while subprime lending came to be characterized by speculation, that is, an attempt by a loan issuer to earn a quick profit while passing along any risk associated with the loan.

One type of lending is sustainable while the other too often results in default. To illuminate how banks might lend sustainably to lower income people, we present two borrowers, Eddie, a CAP participant, and Tonya, who obtained her mortgage from a subprime lender. Eddie is a composite based on the typical CAP borrower. Tonya's story is based on research into the workings of the subprime lending industry.

A Tale of Two Borrowers

Eddie Taylor is a thirty-nine-year-old white man who works in retail sales; his thirty-seven-year-old wife, Laura, works part time in a day care center. Between them, Eddie and Laura earn $37,800 a year. In 2001, just before the birth of their child, the couple obtained a CAP loan through their bank, which had created a special homeownership program for low- and moderate-income households. Eddie and Laura's credit scores were close to 690, and the couple put down $3,300 for their new $111,000 home in the Charlotte area of North Carolina; this gave them a loan-to-value ratio at origination of 97 percent. Their thirty-year, fixed-rate loan carries an interest rate of 7 percent, and the monthly mortgage payment is $717, or 23 percent of the couple's pre-tax income.

The Taylors made it through the highest risk period of homeownership, since owners are most likely to default in the first seven years after they buy. Eddie and Laura passed that milestone and weathered the housing market crisis well. They've seen their home's value appreciate by an average of 1.37 percent a year, though annual gains before the market collapse in mid-2006 exceeded their more recent gains.

Community Advantage Program Product Requirements

Maximum loan-to-value ratio: 97 percent is the typical maximum loan-to-value ratio, though some programs will issue loans for the full value of the home (and one program will issue 103 percent of the value of the home in order to cover closing costs and prepaid items).

Combined loan-to-value (CLTV) ratio: If two loans are used, about 30 percent of programs will allow a loan-to-value ratio of up to 105 percent. Most other programs restrict the CLTV to 103 percent, though some CAP programs restrict CLTV to 97 percent. The junior liens are often provided through subsidized community lending programs and have features such as low interest rates or being forgiven altogether.

Borrower contribution/required down payment: These vary quite a bit, with several programs basing them on borrower credit score or loan amount. A down payment of 1–3 percent of the home price is not uncommon, nor is a minimum borrower contribution of $500.

Seller contribution: Where sellers are allowed to contribute, it is normal for them to be able to put up 3–6 percent of the purchase price.

Ratios: While traditional lenders have restricted the housing debt-to-income ratio at 28 percent and the total debt-to-income ratio at 36 percent (28/36), CAP's lenders have allowed program participants to exceed this. It is not unusual for CAP's lenders to allow a housing debt-to-income ratio of up to 35 percent and a total debt-to-income ratio as high as 45 percent. In allowing these higher ratios, lenders considered a borrower's track record of making similar rental payments.

Credit history: A small number of programs don't require a credit score at all. Some of CAP's lenders allow credit scores as low as 580, and still others require a minimum credit score of 620 or 640. In order to approve qualified lower income borrowers, CAP's lenders take into account undocumented income and nontraditional credit histories.

Eligibility: To qualify for purchase under the CAP program, a loan must be made to a borrower who meets one of three criteria: have income of no more than 80 percent of the area median income (AMI), be a minority with income not in excess of 115 percent of

(continued)

AMI, or purchase a home in a high-minority (>30 percent) or low-income (median income <80 percent of AMI) census tract and have income not in excess of 115 percent of AMI.

Reserves: While half of CAP's lenders have no reserve requirements, the other half require that borrowers hold one or two months' mortgage funds in reserve.

Homebuyer education: Many CAP lenders require homebuyer education; 41 percent of borrowers underwent some form of pre-purchase counseling.

Despite the vagaries of the housing market, by the end of 2009 the home that Eddie and Laura bought for $111,000 in 2001 was worth almost $124,000. With this appreciation, their original down payment, and paying down their mortgage balance by roughly $11,300, their $3,300 investment had grown to $27,600 in equity.

In contrast to this scenario, we introduce Tonya Hinton. Tonya is a thirty-two-year-old African American woman studying for a nursing degree. To support herself while she completes her studies, Tonya works as a certified nursing assistant and earns $24,000 a year. Like the majority of African Americans who obtained a mortgage in 2006, when Tonya bought her Memphis, Tennessee, home that year she used a subprime loan to do so. Tonya could have borrowed from a prime lender since her 695 credit score was slightly better than the Taylors'. However, she relied upon a mortgage broker who advertised in her church's weekly bulletin to help her find suitable housing finance.

Tonya's $96,000 loan was for the full value of her home, and like many subprime mortgages issued that year, it didn't require her to document her income fully. Roughly 90 percent of the subprime loans made between 2004 and 2006 came with exploding interest rates, and Tonya's was no different. Her initial interest rate was 7 percent, which meant that for the first two years of homeownership, her monthly mortgage payment was $639, or 32 percent of her pretax income.

Tonya's broker assured her that she could refinance into a lower cost mortgage before her introductory interest rate expired, but when

Tonya looked into doing so, she discovered that her mortgage came with a prohibitive prepayment fee, which effectively prevented her from refinancing. In the third year of her mortgage, Tonya's interest rate rose to 12 percent and her monthly payment increased to $987, nearly half of her pretax income.

As Tonya struggled to keep current on her mortgage, she restricted her budget to essential expenses. She reduced her driving and began to take public transportation. She no longer ate out and started buying generic groceries whenever possible. She got rid of her cable package, stopped going out to movies, and only got together with friends in their homes. For a while it looked as if Tonya might be able to manage her monthly mortgage payments, but then her fall tuition came due and in August she required emergency dental care for a broken tooth. The combined expenses pushed her budget beyond its limits, and in September of 2009 Tonya missed her mortgage payment, the first time in her life she had ever been delinquent on a bill.

In late September, Tonya received a letter from her loan servicer informing her that her mortgage payment was past due. In October, after two missed payments, the servicer began calling regularly, and Tonya stopped answering the phone. When Tonya missed her third payment in November, she received a "Notice to Accelerate," informing her that she had thirty days to bring her mortgage current or foreclosure proceedings would begin. Tonya did not have the $2,961 that would bring her mortgage up to date, though she did have the $987 she owed for December. Unfortunately, the servicer refused to take anything but full payment of all amounts owed. Tonya was not surprised when she came home a week before Christmas to find a notice of foreclosure taped to her front door. The public trustee's sale date was set for early February, and Tonya used the time between Christmas and the sale date to find a rental she could afford.

How else has Tonya's life been affected by the foreclosure process? Besides losing her home and the $1,700 she put into maintenance and upgrades during her first three years living there, Tonya had to move away from a neighborhood she loved and from neighbors she relied on and cared about. For her, that was the more significant loss. Because she was behind in her mortgage and so couldn't pass a credit check, Tonya couldn't rent in any of the nicer apartment complexes in the Memphis area. Instead, she is now living in a small garage apartment near her nursing school.

Tonya's work life has also been affected. After the agency where she had worked for three years as a certified nursing assistant closed, Tonya was unable to obtain a new job since one of the conditions for employment at the several agencies she applied to was maintenance of a good credit record. It took Tonya several months to find a job where her credit record would not be checked as a condition of employment, and she had to withdraw from school in order to work sufficient hours to recoup her lost income. Tonya now works for a family taking care of their elderly grandmother who suffers from Alzheimer's. Her employers know about her recent housing woes, but they do not think that these problems reflect poorly on Tonya's reliability.

Tonya's financial life has been devastated. Following the default, her credit score dropped from 695 to 520, and the interest rates on her credit cards soared as a result, in one case from 17 to 28 percent. She is finding it difficult to pay down the balances that accrued when her mortgage rate rose and her monthly cost of living increased. Tonya knows that her housing, employment, and credit opportunities will be constrained for the seven-year period that the default stays on her credit record. The stress she experienced as a result of the foreclosure, job loss, and credit woes has made her wary of borrowing, and she no longer wants to own a home.

We now come to the heart of the question: what went right for Eddie and Laura, who were able to accumulate $27,600 in equity during a time when many lower income and minority homeowners, like Tonya, were forced into foreclosure?

Access to Credit

The first thing that went right for Eddie and Laura was that they had access to affordable housing finance. As we explain in chapter 2, the Community Reinvestment Act of 1977 was created to promote the flow of credit to banks' entire service areas, including the regions where lower income and minority customers are concentrated. The Federal Reserve estimates that the CRA has "leveraged . . . $4.5 trillion in these communities and helped to create jobs, develop small businesses, and make mortgages accessible."[1]

CRA lending has played two critical roles in the mortgage-lending arena. First, it has helped increase the availability of affordable credit, as our analysis of Self-Help's CAP demonstrates. We find that before 2002, the year when subprime credit became increasingly available to lower income homeowners, seventy-five of every hundred CAP loans would not have been originated without CAP's underlying affordable lending programs. Second, more recently community reinvestment lending has actually helped keep borrowers out of troublesome subprime loans. Our research shows that between 2004 and 2006, when the subprime market was flourishing, every hundred new CAP originations resulted in seventy-one fewer high-cost originations.[2]

Before 2002 lower income borrowers faced a dearth of credit; after 2002 lower income borrowers faced a rapacious subprime industry. CAP helped lower income and minority borrowers navigate each of these problems. Community reinvestment mortgage lending not only stimulates the flow of housing credit where the supply would otherwise be limited, it also protects lower income and minority borrowers from becoming mired in high-cost subprime loans. Our analysis clearly demonstrates that community reinvestment and subprime products serve some of the same borrowers. When they have a clear choice, most lower income borrowers will choose affordable, sustainable loans over higher priced, riskier products.

Access to Sustainable Products

Access to credit alone would not have been enough to enable long-term homeownership for Eddie and Laura, however. This brings the discussion to the second thing that went right for the Taylors: they got a mortgage they could afford for the life of the loan. Their bank structured the loan to remain affordable and issued the mortgage only after careful consideration of their ability to repay it.

Eddie and Laura are currently paying down a fixed-rate, thirty-year mortgage, the same type of product that puts the dream of home-ownership within the grasp of many Americans. As we mention in chapter 2, before the long-term, low down payment, fully amortized mortgage was developed in the 1930s, Americans who wanted to own a home had to save up a large down payment and finance the remainder of the home with a short-term mortgage culminating in a balloon payment.

Besides having access to an affordable mortgage, Eddie and Laura benefited from being carefully screened for their ability to afford and manage their mortgage. Their lender required that most of the $3,300 they put down on their home come from their own savings. The couple was required to keep one month's worth of principal, interest, taxes, and insurance funds in reserve to protect them against financial difficulties. Their lender checked Eddie and Laura's credit history for late payments and bankruptcies and provided guidelines for redressing any outstanding problems with their credit. Before issuing the loan, the lender required the couple to complete a prepurchase homebuyer education program.

Just a few years ago, this careful screening on the part of a lending institution would have seemed like an unprofitable use of time, a process contrary to what had become the efficient, highly automated business of issuing credit. Americans now know, however, that an initial investment of diligence pays off in the long run: when lenders fail to ensure that borrowers can afford to repay their loans over time, the results are ultimately exceedingly costly, both for lending institutions and for the broader public who foot the bill for years of reckless lending.

Tonya's mortgage, in contrast to Eddie and Laura's and like so much subprime lending, was not affordable for the long term and therefore did not allow her to remain in her home. Like many subprime loans, Tonya's mortgage came with an affordable introductory rate that adjusted beyond her means after two years. Her lender issued her mortgage without assessing whether Tonya could afford it after the interest rate reset. The mortgage came with a prepayment penalty that Tonya could not afford and that effectively kept her from refinancing.

When we analyze the CAP portfolio, we find that community reinvestment mortgage lending provides people with loans that they can afford and sustain over the long term. But is that because CAP loans were made only to less-risky borrowers? How, we wondered, do CAP borrowers compare with subprime borrowers in terms of their risk characteristics?

To answer this question, we compared the loan performance of CAP borrowers with that of comparable low- and moderate-income borrowers holding subprime loans. The comparison used performance information from the for-profit company Lender Processing Services, Inc. (LPS, formerly McDash Analytics), which has an extensive database on active first and second mortgages. Relying on propensity score-matching methods to pair borrowers, the performance differences of CAP and subprime borrowers could be attributed to nothing other than their mortgage terms or the channels through which they got their loans. To make sure the loans themselves were roughly similar, CAP loans were compared only to subprime, first-lien, single-family purchase mortgages, with full or alternative documentation, issued during the same period.

Our research is groundbreaking in several ways. First, while earlier studies focus on how the same mortgages performed in different markets, our focus is on similar borrowers with different mortgages, allowing us to compare the relative risk attributable to different mortgage products. Second, because it is difficult to identify community reinvestment loans in the publicly available loan data sets, research on the performance of CRA loans is scarce. The CAP data set provides us with a unique opportunity to study the long-term viability of CRA-type products. Third, the use of propensity score models addresses the selection bias issue—that is, the chance that performance differences might be due to differences in the borrowers who select CAP or subprime loans—and constructs a comparison group based on observational data; this allows us to isolate the impact of loan product features and origination channel on the performance of mortgages.

In our analysis, we consider the impact of one origination channel (brokers) and two loan characteristics (the prepayment penalty and the adjustable rate). We constructed six mutually exclusive variables for the combinations of these three characteristics. None of the CAP loans have these features, and so we used them as the reference group in our models.

We discovered that, for comparable borrowers, those with community reinvestment loans are much less likely to default than those with subprime mortgages. Consistently, subprime loans turned out to have a higher default risk than CAP loans. The estimated cumulative default rate of the subprime loans issued in 2004 is 16.3 percent, about four times the default rate (4.1 percent) of CAP loans issued in the same year. For a 2006 subprime loan, the cumulative default rate is over 47 percent, about 3.5 times that of comparable CAP loans (13.3 percent). In other words, a CAP loan is over 70 percent less likely to default than a comparable subprime loan across vintages.

We also find that subprime loans with both adjustable interest rates and prepayment penalties have a substantially higher default risk than loans without these traits. For a retail-originated subprime adjustable-rate mortgage without prepayment penalty, the estimated cumulative default rate would be 6.5 percent, slightly higher than that of a CAP loan (4.1 percent). But if the adjustable-rate subprime mortgage has a prepayment penalty, the estimated default rate doubles to 13.5 percent.

Where borrowers got their loans turns out to matter a great deal too. We find that those who used mortgage brokers were three to five times more likely to default than those who borrowed through other channels, all things being equal. When borrowers used a broker and took out an adjustable-rate loan or a loan with a prepayment penalty, their default risk was even higher. And in the worst scenario, when broker origination is combined with an adjustable rate and a prepayment penalty, the borrower's default risk was four to five times as high as that of a comparable borrower holding an affordable CRA mortgage.[3]

These results convinced us that the higher default rate of subprime loans is not necessarily attributable to the credit risk profile of the borrowers. Instead, it is due to the characteristics of the loans themselves and also the channel through which the loans originated. Our analysis helped us realize that, when structured correctly and responsibly, lending to low- and moderate-income borrowers is a viable proposition.

Our composite characters Eddie and Tonya highlight this point: their experiences were very different but not because they were very different as borrowers. They were equally creditworthy and equally willing to work hard to achieve homeownership. Instead, their outcomes were so different because the loans they used to purchase their homes were so different. This point deserves particular emphasis, because Eddie and Tonya stand in for the millions of Americans who bought homes during the recent housing boom.

Wanting to find out more about how loan characteristics affect borrowers' ability to repay, we decided to look more carefully at predatory loans. Predatory loans contain features that other subprime and prime loans don't, features that raise borrowing costs or the risk of default while providing no countervailing benefits to the borrower.[4] In other words, predatory lenders convince borrowers—sometimes through illegal practices—to take out mortgages that can do them financial harm. Predatory lenders may underwrite a loan based on the value of the collateral rather than on the borrower's ability to repay. They may induce a borrower to refinance repeatedly for no other reason than to generate additional points and fees for the lender (loan flipping). They may engage in fraud and deception to conceal from an unsuspecting or unsophisticated borrower the true nature and cost of the loan obligation.[5]

Predatory loans might include costly prepayment penalties—often in effect for an extended period—that prevent borrowers from refinancing when interest rates fall (or before the loan's interest rate resets) or when a borrower's credit record improves. They may also have balloon payments that exceed a borrower's ability to pay when they fall due, forcing yet another refinancing and new round of fees and charges. To assess the impact of these two attributes in particular, we examined over 120,000 loans to see if balloon payments and prepayment penalties increase the likelihood of foreclosure once other risk factors are taken into account. We find that these predatory loan features lead to a significant increase in mortgage foreclosure risk, all else being equal.[6] For instance, refinance loans with prepayment penalties and those with balloon payments are more likely to experience a foreclosure than are loans without these characteristics—by about 20 percent and 50 percent, respectively. Furthermore, we estimate that the use of prepayment penalties and balloon payment requirements in 1999 refinance originations alone increased foreclosure-related losses nationally by about $465 and $127 million, respectively. Our findings suggest that predatory loans have the potential not only to erode household wealth but also to heighten the negative impacts of foreclosure on individuals, households, and communities.

While there is no doubt that the impact of the subprime foreclosure crisis was widespread, researchers are learning that the crisis hit minorities disproportionally. As of the fourth quarter of 2009, 43 percent of subprime adjustable-rate mortgages across the United States were either ninety days or more delinquent or in the process of foreclosure (that is, "seriously delinquent"). Fixed-rate subprime loans weren't performing much better—some 22 percent of these loans were seriously delinquent.[7] But although most subprime loans went to whites, blacks across the United States were almost three times more likely than whites to receive a subprime first-lien home loan, and Hispanics were more than twice as likely as whites to do so.

Besides being more likely to have a subprime loan, minority homeowners tend to have a higher proportion of their wealth concentrated in their homes than whites do. Consequently, the potential wealth loss associated with the subprime crisis affects these homeowners disproportionately. After years of exclusion from financing opportunities, this loss constitutes a devastating injustice. By one estimate, minority homeowners who obtained subprime loans between 1998 and 2006 are slated to lose a minimum of $164 billion in household wealth due to the mortgage finance crisis.[8] This astounding figure masks the thousands of individual minority families whose wealth has been wiped out, whose access to affordable credit has been curtailed, and whose hopes of a better future for themselves and their children have been thwarted.

As Tonya's experience illustrates, losing a home has effects beyond loss of wealth. Homeowners who undergo foreclosure will find their credit scores devastated and can expect the foreclosure to appear on their credit report for up to seven years. This will affect their access to credit, the cost of the credit they obtain, their job prospects, their access to housing, and their access to finance for education and, thereby, their educational opportunities.

The losses associated with the subprime mortgage crisis extend beyond the borrowers who have lost or will lose their homes. The International Monetary Fund estimates the global effect of the U.S. mortgage crisis on banks, hedge funds, pension systems, and other investments at $1.4 trillion. Here in the United States, interbank lending largely froze following revelations that banks were carrying large amounts of toxic assets (that is, subprime mortgage loans) on their books. Despite the taxpayer dollars pumped into the U.S. financial sector through the Troubled Assets Relief Program (TARP), estimates are that the volume of outstanding loans at America's largest financial institutions fell at an 8.8 percent annual rate during the final quarter of 2008 alone.[9] The value of American residential real estate fell by $7 trillion between 2005 and mid-2009.[10]

Lending done the wrong way devastates individuals, communities, banks, and the economy. In sharp contrast to this, lending that is consistent with the safe and sound operation of financial institutions has an entirely different effect. As of the fourth quarter of 2009 only 7.6 percent of CAP loans were ninety days or more delinquent. At that point, subprime loans had four times that level of serious delinquency. Considering the depressed state of the market and the limited resources of these households, this is remarkable. In fact, as of that time some 68 percent of CAP's low-income borrowers had never been even thirty days delinquent on their mortgage payments, a testimony to the success of affordable lending when it is done with long-term homeownership as its primary goal.

A Decent Long-Term Investment

The third thing that went right for Eddie and Laura was that their affordable home was a decent investment over the long run. Here, Tonya and the Taylors have something in common: Tonya also chose a home that would appreciate over time. However, because of the way her mortgage was structured, Tonya could not realize these gains.

As we note in chapter 2, homeowners build wealth through their homes in two ways: first, by reaping the return associated with house price appreciation (if there is any), and second, through the forced savings mechanism of mortgage payments. Our examination of CAP borrowers finds that they have fared well in terms of house price appreciation, despite tumultuous shifts in the real estate market. From loan origination through the second quarter of 2009, CAP homeowners saw their homes go up in value by a median annualized rate of 2.5 percent.

In comparison, during that same period, the Dow Jones Industrial Average declined by 3.4 percent on an annualized basis, and six-month certificates of deposit (CD) averaged an annual return of 3.4 percent. It's true that investing in a CD might have brought greater returns in the short run, but there are two advantages to investing one's money in a home. First, you can't live in a CD. A home is a consumption good and is therefore an investment that also provides the tangible benefits of an inviolable shelter. Second, homeownership is a unique opportunity for leveraged investment: an owner puts down only a fraction of the value of the home on purchase but gains any increase in its overall value at resale.

Of course, some suggest that affordable homeownership has drawbacks as a wealth-building tool. They speculate, first, that investing in the home leaves lower income homeowners with few resources for other investments, resulting in an underdiversified portfolio.[11] Second, they think lower income homeowners may be likely to deplete their housing wealth by overborrowing against their equity.[12]

We used the CAP data to assess the legitimacy of these criticisms. We focused our investigation on two questions. First, are homeowners increasing their borrowing as they accumulate home equity? Second, are homeowners limiting their investments in other financial instruments—that is, does investment in the home result in lower income owners having underdiversified portfolios?

Our analysis involved estimating the relationships between equity accumulation and the major components of the households' financial portfolios. While we find some association between the accumulation of large amounts of equity—over about $150,000—and increased indebtedness (between 10 and 30 percent of that amount), overall, we find no evidence that debt accumulation offsets the wealth-building effects of equity accumulation. We also find no evidence of shortfalls in alternative investments or savings resulting from the accumulation of equity; that is, we do not find that investment in the home crowds out other investments. Generally speaking, our analysis provides evidence that community reinvestment lending serves as an effective means for promoting stable wealth building for lower income households through the forced-savings mechanism of equity accumulation.[13]

What impact have equity gains had on the wealth of CAP's participating families? Since CAP families enjoyed a median annualized home appreciation rate of 2.5 percent, they experienced a median equity increase of $21,400. These gains amount to an annualized return on equity of an astounding 32 percent!

When CAP borrowers bought their homes matters, of course. We find that homeowners who bought earlier fared better than those who bought more recently, with the median 1998 buyer seeing a 43 percent increase in house value as opposed to the 2 percent median gain experienced by those who bought in 2004. And as is always the case with real estate, location matters. For instance, the median CAP buyer in California saw her equity increase by $84,500, while the median buyer in Michigan saw his equity increase by only $5,100. These gains stand despite an average house price decline of 27 percent in California and 23 percent in Michigan between 2004 and 2009.

Servicing Matters

The fourth factor contributing to the differences in Tonya's and the Taylors' homeownership experiences is the practices of their respective servicers.

Loan servicers collect mortgage payments from borrowers and disburse them to lenders, investors, local governments, and insurers. Servicers send payment notices and year-end tax statements to borrowers and tax authorities. They administer escrow accounts that cover real estate property taxes and hazard insurance. They contact borrowers who have fallen behind in their payments and initiate foreclosure proceedings against delinquent borrowers. Loan servicers also collect and report payment information to national credit bureaus, act as the customer support agent for the lender, and handle interest rate adjustments on adjustable-rate mortgages.[14]

This long list of responsibilities makes clear that servicers have enormous influence over the smooth functioning of a mortgage. The list also illustrates that servicers have a great deal of power over what happens to a mortgage when a borrower falls behind in his payments. In essence, servicers have the power to turn a delinquency into a default.

Fortunately for Eddie and Laura, their loan servicing company works proactively to assist borrowers who fall behind in their payments. In 2004, just three years into owning their new home, Eddie and Laura needed to pay expenses related to their daughter's delayed speech development, something not covered under the couple's insurance plan. The Taylors found themselves forced to choose between obtaining care and services for their daughter and making their mortgage payment on time. They chose the former and missed their February mortgage payment.

Because their servicing agency actively addresses delinquency, Eddie and Laura received a call just eight days after missing their payment. Their servicer referred the couple to a counselor who helped them negotiate a plan that would allow them to catch up on their loan payments. The Taylors opted for a "partial reinstatement," whereby they resumed regular mortgage payments in March and made good on the missed payment by May. While they did have to pay a late fee, Eddie and Laura were current on their mortgage again within three months of the missed payment. The Taylors' experience is not unusual. When low- and moderate-income homeowners who are behind on their mortgage payments participate in a repayment plan, they are 68 percent less likely to lose their home.[15]

How do loan servicing methods affect loan performance? We used the CAP data to find out. We analyzed 15,038 periods of delinquency experienced by 5,886 borrowers, which comes to an average of 2.6 delinquency spells per loan. All these episodes ended in either cure or default by December 2004—some 85 percent ended with the borrower catching up on payments, while 15 percent ended in default.

Our goal was to identify factors that predict the likelihood that a given delinquency will either cure or default, and so we controlled for various characteristics that might affect delinquency outcomes. The first were loan characteristics, including level of home equity, loan age, and the number of previous delinquencies. Second, we controlled for borrower characteristics, such as total debt-to-income ratios of 38 percent or higher, income as a percentage of area median income, gender, race/ethnicity, first-time home-buyer status, and credit score. Third, we controlled for economic conditions, including the estimated annual rate of appreciation for each property. Finally, we incorporated variables for the eight main loan servicers to test for differences among them.

Our analysis reveals that when low- and moderate-income borrowers fall behind in their mortgage payments, the loan servicer can have a substantial impact on the likelihood of cure or default and foreclosure. Specifically, we find that, after controlling for loan characteristics, borrower characteristics, and economic conditions, the specific loan servicer can reduce the odds of a delinquent loan's curing by between 20 and 40 percent.[16]

Our findings suggest a need for policymakers to encourage servicing practices that emphasize early intervention in order to help troubled borrowers avoid foreclosure. Proactive efforts to avoid foreclosure don't just benefit homeowners, they also benefit lenders, whose costs increase as delinquency lapses into serious delinquency and then into foreclosure. During this process, lenders bear the opportunity cost of principal and income not received, servicing costs, legal costs, costs of property preservation, and costs of property disposition.

The Center for Responsible Lending has estimated the price of fore-closure at $50,000 per home, an amount that includes processing fees, liquidation sale price cuts, and other expenses.[17]

Unlike other players in the lending process, the loan servicer does not normally lose money on a foreclosure and may even make money by charging fees during the foreclosure process. Unfortunately, they are usually unable to recoup all the costs associated with reworking and salvaging the loan. This misalignment of incentives, where lenders and homeowners might benefit from curing a loan but servicers, who have the actual power to determine whether or not to foreclose, benefit from foreclosure, is something that affordable housing policy must address. We return to this point in chapter 6.

Building a Better Future

Clearly, Tonya and the Taylors did not fare equally well in their first forays into homeownership. Tonya's default and foreclosure devas-tated her credit record and will affect her housing, employment, and borrowing opportunities for years. Worse, perhaps, losing her home was such an emotional, financial, and psychological blow that Tonya has no desire to attempt homeownership again.

Eddie and Laura, on the other hand, took the first successful steps toward building wealth through homeownership. Wealth gains are not the only benefit of their becoming and remaining owners, how-ever: as they continue to pay down their mortgage successfully, their credit scores will improve, increasing their access to further affordable finance. While this might seem like an obvious result of being a reli-able borrower, in fact it has not been well researched to date.

To fill this gap, we examined the credit score trajectories of CAP borrowers. We find that while they do differ substantially, with bor-rower wealth, race/ethnicity, the presence of children, and self-reported thriftiness each being consistently associated with changes in credit rat-ing in the years following home purchase, the demographic patterns are moderated by the inclusion of borrowers' payment history. We find that in fact if you pay down your mortgage reliably, your credit score will improve, while if you fail to do so, your credit score might be devastated. What might be surprising is what we learned about the potential effect of a single missed payment on one's credit score: the credit scores of lower income borrowers who remain current on their mortgage payments are between 70 and 80 points higher than those who miss just one month's payment.

Of course, an individual's credit score and documented credit history reinforce each other. Payment history affects credit score, credit score affects cost and quality of credit, and cost and quality of credit affects one's ability to pay down credit, which affects credit score. But the individual choices borrowers make about credit use and payment are not the only things that affect their credit history. To the extent that one's credit history reflects one's economic position, building good credit requires more than simply the resolve to make payments on time. Instead, it likely requires a job with health insurance benefits, a low likelihood of layoff or unemployment, and other amenities that create economic security among advantaged groups. There is no doubt that poorly underwritten loans are ultimately harmful to borrowers. Although high-cost loans may seem beneficial in the short term, because they allow households with limited resources to enter home-ownership, they have been shown to be unsustainable in the long run.

In contrast, our research offers further evidence that community reinvestment lending sets owners on a path of sustainable homeownership and long-term prosperity. In fact, between seven and eleven years after buying their homes, 85 percent of all owners in the study, and 86 percent of the minority households, remained homeowners. Contrary to assertions that low-income and minority homeowners are more likely to exit homeownership and return to renting, and that these groups are therefore less likely to benefit from the long-term gains associated with homeownership, we find that CAP homeowners develop a "taste for ownership."

We determined this by pairing homeowners holding subprime mortgages with those holding community reinvestment products and examining how long CAP borrowers in different racial and income categories maintained homeowner status. We find that lower income and minority homeowners are in fact less likely than their higher income and white counterparts to move, but no less likely to purchase a new home when a move is made.[18] Our findings challenge those of earlier studies that include a preponderance of subprime mortgages in the study populations. We believe our research more accurately predicts the potential for sustained homeownership among the populations targeted by community reinvestment and other affordable lending programs.

However, when community reinvestment borrowers choose to refinance their loans, some do make costly mistakes. When we look at CAP borrowers who refinanced, we find that while 80 percent chose fixed-rate mortgages, the other 20 percent opted for adjustable-rate mortgages. Both sets of borrowers originally held CAP mortgages, with interest rates averaging 7.6 percent, and refinanced into products with interest rates that averaged just below 6.0 percent.[19]

Among the refinances we examined, 66 percent refinanced solely to secure a lower interest rate, while the remaining 34 percent extracted equity in the process. Borrowers who extracted equity told us they used it for a wide range of purposes: 61 percent used it primarily to pay off credit card balances or other debts, and 27 percent used it primarily for home improvement or home repair. The remaining 12 percent used it for educational expenses, medical debts, and vehicle down payments, among other things.

While the majority of refinancing CAP borrowers secured lower cost prime loans, some 15 percent of borrowers who refinanced received higher cost mortgages (loans with an interest rate that exceeds the prime rate by 150 basis points or more). Why, we wondered, would these borrowers choose to transition to subprime loans? To find out, we examined the differences between those who refinanced for a lower interest rate (rate refinancing) and those who refinanced to extract equity from their homes (cash-out refinancing). It turns out that borrowers chose different loan products according to whether they were motivated by rate or cash-out refinancing. While rate refinancing is driven by the financial incentive to secure a lower interest rate, cash-out refinancing confronts borrowers with the trade-off between the long-term cost of the mortgage, the monthly payment obligation, and the ability to extract equity to meet some need.

Within the CAP sample, we find this trade-off appears to lead a subset of borrowers to refinance into adjustable-rate loans in order to extract equity while minimizing the monthly payment obligation in the short term. Equity extraction is strongly associated with the likelihood of refinancing into an ARM product, and the effect is concentrated among the households most likely to be constrained by payment-to-income requirements. In essence, the desire to extract equity led some households to accept subprime credit in exchange for lower monthly payment obligations and the ability to extract equity.[20] The need to extract equity will lead a minority of community reinvestment borrowers to refinance into subprime products unless policymakers focus on promoting the availability of affordable loans for homeowners who find themselves in an economic pinch.

Despite these findings, the majority of community reinvestment borrowers who subsequently refinanced did so into fixed-rate loans at lower interest rates than their original mortgages. Likewise, the majority of those who sold the homes they bought with CAP mortgages and bought another home took out a fixed-rate loan to do so. On average, those who bought a subsequent home have more equity than those who stayed in their original homes, which indicates that community reinvestment lending can be a jumping-off point for wealth creation.

Wealth creation is not the only benefit experienced by CAP families, though. Despite current economic conditions, the majority of CAP homeowners who were surveyed in the depth of the crisis in 2009 report that they are satisfied overall with their homeownership experiences. In particular, 86 percent of current homeowners report that they would be somewhat likely (31 percent) or very likely (55 percent) to purchase their current homes again if they had the opportunity to go back in time and revisit that decision. Moreover, the majority report that they find paying their mortgages and maintaining their homes "not at all stressful." Eighty percent of respondents report having financial reserves greater than or equal to twice the amount of their mortgage payments, and only a small subset of respondents (9 percent) report significant financial or other stress related to their homes.

These are benefits that borrowers like Tonya Hinton, who obtained a subprime loan, have so far been denied. Existing policy has not yet enabled Tonya and millions like her to make a sustainable entry into homeownership. In fact, it has left them open to the unscrupulous tactics of subprime lenders and left them further behind financially. The majority of these borrowers, though viable, are seldom served by the mainstream financial market. Were it not for community reinvestment initiatives like CAP, the benefits of affordable homeownership might elude them altogether.

How do we ensure that the path to an affordable mortgage and so to a better life—through economic mobility for both the homeowner and the next generation—is open to all who can repay that mortgage, given half a chance? We take up this question in chapter 6. First, though, we delve more deeply into the experience of CAP borrowers during these troubled economic times.

5 | *Stress Testing Community Reinvestment Lending*

The Community Advantage Program study began as an effort to examine whether lending to lower income borrowers was a viable undertaking, from the perspectives of the lending institutions, the secondary market, and the borrower households. However, the continuing economic crisis has given us the chance to assess the costs and benefits of lower income homeownership not just in a time of steady house price gains but also throughout a full business cycle, including a dramatic economic downturn.

Having followed thousands of lower income homeowners closely, we were in an ideal position to assess precisely how such owners were affected by the crisis and what they were doing to weather it. About two years into the crisis, we began asking CAP homeowners detailed questions about how they were managing the economic challenges they faced. Had they lost work? Had their wealth decreased? Were they still in their homes? If they were keeping up with their mortgage payments, how were they managing to do so? Were they tapping into retirement savings? Had they dropped health insurance or decreased their level of health care? Were they taking on additional debt? How were the stresses of the crisis affecting them and their housing decisions?

The crisis didn't change what is important to our research, but it increased the research's relevance to those policymakers currently engaged in debates about the desirability of promoting affordable homeownership. What we are learning during the recession can help them determine what approaches are most effective in supporting homeowners through financial challenges. The experiences of CAP borrowers show what actually happens when those who have received affordable loans find themselves under financial stress. Consequently, the evidence we're gathering provides useful information about both how to move forward out of the economic crisis and also how to avoid another mortgage meltdown.

How CAP Families Are Weathering the Crisis

In 2008 the CAP survey included questions about participants' levels of psychological stress, financial stress, and satisfaction with their financial situation. The following year the survey included the same questions as well as new questions about their housing experiences. Our analysis of these data focuses on several important questions. Were homeowners experiencing more stress—either financial or psychological—since the recession began? If so, what caused that stress? How were differently situated households coping with financial stress? What choices and trade-offs were households facing, and what role did tenure (homeownership versus renting) play in the experience of lower income households in a tumultuous economic environment?

On a practical level, most current CAP homeowners are weathering the crisis relatively well. As we have already discussed, on average, CAP homeowners demonstrate robust wealth gains and good loan performance, despite recent economic conditions. What survey respondents report about their ability to manage their mortgages corroborates what is revealed through other means. When the default rate for prime borrowers with adjustable-rate mortgages are compared with what many would say are subprime borrowers in our community reinvestment portfolio, it is clear that prime borrowers were doing worse than CAP community reinvestment borrowers: the rate of serious delinquency for adjustable rate prime borrowers is 18 percent, while for CAP borrowers, it is less than half this—7.6 percent.[1]

CAP mortgages generally outperform subprime mortgages, both for similar borrowers and overall. As of the end of 2009 the CAP ninety-day serious delinquency rate of 7.6 percent was below the comparable rates for subprime fixed-rate (22 percent) and adjustable-rate (43 percent) mortgages, which increased by 62 percent and 26 percent, respectively, between 2008 and 2009.[2] By the middle of 2009, about 12 percent of nonprime loans originated nationally between 2000 and 2007 had gone through foreclosure.[3] In contrast, cumulative CAP foreclosure sales reached 4.2 percent at the end of 2009, up from 3.7 percent at the end of 2008.

Mortgage performance is only one measure of how well lower income homeowners are faring during these difficult economic times. Another measure is owners' economic security. CAP homeowners report feeling economically secure, with more than half of them reporting that they have not been adversely affected by the economic crisis and 70 percent saying that their financial situation has either stayed the same or improved within the last year. Although some 60 percent of owners report that they are thriftier in their financial habits and 44 percent say that they postponed home repairs, 70 percent report that they are partly or completely satisfied with their financial situations. Further, some 53 percent say that they put aside additional savings during the year. While 30 percent report dissatisfaction with their overall financial situations, only 10 percent state that they found managing their money very stressful. Few filed for bankruptcy (2 percent), used payday loans (3.5 percent), or tapped retirement savings (6 percent).

What of CAP homeowners who did report financial difficulties? We probed further into the data to determine why they were experiencing these problems, what they were doing to stay afloat, and what measures might make the most difference in helping them through these troubling financial times.

Of the homeowners who still lived in their original CAP home as of 2008 and who responded to both the 2008 and 2009 surveys, 315 (16 percent) report both a decline in their financial circumstances during the past year and current dissatisfaction with their finances. Of those who fell into this group, 73 percent report having negative equity in their homes, and 12 percent say they tried unsuccessfully to sell their houses. In addition, approximately 40 percent experienced a reduction in household income, with a median decrease of $10,000 (about 20 percent of household income).

In only 6 percent of these 315 financially strained households did the respondent or spouse go from being employed to unemployed between the 2008 and 2009 interviews, but 34 percent of respondents and 26 percent of spouses report a reduction in working hours. In addition, 60 percent report a major unexpected expense, such as medical or vet bills, a significant home or car repair, or legal costs. As of the 2009 interview, 30 percent of those who incurred such an expense still owed money on it.[4]

About a third of the 315 homeowners who report both a decline in their financial circumstances during the past year and current dissatisfaction with their finances postponed their house payment at some point; half of them say that they did so due to job loss.[5] Some 40 percent of owners who delayed payment cite money management problems as the reason for missing their mortgage payment. Although a small number of financially straitened owners resorted to filing bankruptcy, far more of them addressed their situations through increased use of discount stores (63 percent), by borrowing from family (41 percent), and by postponing paying bills (58 percent), receiving medical care (46 percent), and paying housing-related expenses (79 percent). Only 1 percent report having been removed from their homes in 2009 due to delinquent payments.

Homeownership in Difficult Times

How are CAP homeowners managing homeownership during the financial crisis? In order to consider this question, we compare four groups of owners: those who, between the 2008 survey and the 2009 survey, kept and remained in their property; those who kept the property but moved elsewhere; those who sold their home and purchased a new home; and those who transitioned to renting. The vast majority of owners (92 percent) who lived in their original CAP property in

2008 remained there through 2009. Just 4 percent (thirty-eight owners) moved to a new residence but kept their CAP home. Another 3
percent (thirty owners) sold their CAP home and purchased a new
residence, while 1 percent (ten owners) sold their CAP home and transitioned to renting.[6]

Those CAP homeowners who sold their properties and bought
other properties during the 2008–09 period report the most positive
experience. They were much less likely to report having reduced
expenses, becoming unemployed, missing payments, experiencing foreclosure, or facing credit constraints. Interestingly, even though they are
the least likely to feel dissatisfied with their financial situation and
least likely to feel they had too much debt, they are by far the most
likely to feel they had too much mortgage (50 percent reported feeling
thus).

A second group of owners, those who moved and either purchased
or rented another home but also kept their CAP homes, are in general
younger than the other groups who remained owners. They are less
likely to be employed than those who stayed in their CAP homes, are
the most likely to have had their credit limit reduced, and are the most
likely to have borrowed from friends and family. They report the most
stress over paying their mortgage and rent, perhaps because they found
it a challenge to juggle two properties. Negative equity appears to be
a key factor in families moving away from their CAP properties, with
CAP owners who stayed in their homes being the least likely of all
groups to have negative equity.

Those who transitioned from owning to renting between 2008 and
2009 actually report a decrease in both financial and general stress.
They are the least likely to feel they were paying too much for their
housing, but half feel they had too much debt overall. Back in 2008,
when these individuals were still owners, they reported the highest
level of financial stress and had a higher share of negative equity. More
of them became unemployed (20 percent) and declared bankruptcy (20
percent). The combination of these factors suggests that a greater share
of these owners got into financial distress in 2008 and that they experienced some relief once they transitioned to renting.

Though the CAP portfolio has experienced relatively few defaults, as the above analysis shows, some defaults are inevitable. Turning to the issue of default, our data enable research into the decision by low- and moderate-income homeowners to file for bankruptcy. Over the course of the CAP evaluation, the annual rate at which homeowners filed for bankruptcy is slightly higher than for the general population (1.9 percent versus 1.2 percent). We examined motives for filing and find that adverse circumstances increased the likelihood of filing; these include unexpected expenses, unemployment, mortgage delinquencies, lack of health insurance, and difficulty paying medical bills. Despite stereotypes that debtors file for bankruptcy simply to gain a financial advantage, the data reveal that in fact stressors within the household are much more likely to account for bankruptcy filings by CAP homeowners.[7]

Housing and Stress

These findings raise a new question: if homeownership is a drain on the limited resources of lower income families, wouldn't owners be more likely than renters to report feeling financially strained and to report higher levels of stress overall? Fortunately, the CAP data allow us to probe into this question.

Shortly after the first administration of the CAP survey in 2003, it became clear that the CAP data set would be even richer if a sample of renters were added to the study to allow for comparative analysis with the homeowners. Accordingly, a comparison group of renters was matched to the homeowners based on neighborhood proximity and income; this matching was limited to the thirty metropolitan areas in the United States with the highest number of CAP homeowners. Like the CAP homeowners, the renters had an annual income no more than 80 percent of area median income (AMI) if white or no more than 115 percent of AMI if nonwhite. Respondents also had to be between eighteen and sixty-five years old and pay rent to the owner of their residence. We interview these renter households annually.

The renter sample adds a powerful dimension to the CAP study since it allows us to isolate the costs and benefits associated with owning a home. Because people self-select into homeownership, research that assesses the impacts of homeownership can be influenced by endogenous relations among variables. We use statistical techniques to ensure that we do not misinterpret the correlations between tenure choice and the outcomes of interest, typically applying propensity score analysis to minimize the effects of selection before we compare the owner and renter samples. This approach ensures that the households we study are similar, except that some of them own their homes while some of them rent.

In this section we use this comparison group to ask whether households of modest means might see themselves as better off without the responsibilities of owning a home. In this weak real estate market, would lower income families be happier renting than owning?

To examine the relative stress levels of lower income owners and renters, we rely on the responses of homeowners and renters who answered both the 2008 and 2009 surveys. Starting with 2,216 owners and 797 renters, we use coarsened exact matching to extrapolate a small well-matched sample of homeowners and renters. In comparing these lower income renters and owners, we focus on three key outcomes: general stress, financial stress, and overall satisfaction with financial situation. For each, we test whether owning a home in 2008, as opposed to renting, increased or decreased the impact of the recession in 2009.

What does the analysis reveal? First, there is no significant relationship between homeownership and financial stress, even during the economic crisis of 2008–09.[8] Homeowners in the panel are neither more nor less likely than renters similarly situated in terms of age, race, income, dwelling type, and other socioeconomic indicators, to report financial stressors in 2009. However, the homeowners do report feeling less general stress, that is, they are more likely to report feeling in control of important aspects of their lives.[9] Further, lower income CAP homeowners are 60 percent more likely than their renter counterparts to report a higher level of satisfaction with their financial situation.[10]

In sum, though the homeowners in the CAP sample are neither more nor less likely than the renters to have experienced financial stressors during the economic crunch, homeowners exhibit a greater perception of being in control and reported significantly higher financial satisfaction than renters. This suggests that the condition of homeownership somehow provides a greater sense of financial security: although the homeowners and the renters both experienced financial stress to a remarkably similar degree, the homeowners experienced less overall stress than the renters and a greater sense of financial satisfaction. Perhaps homeownership gives people a sense of being in control of their lives that in turn reduces the stress they feel as a result of financial hardships. Whatever the mechanism through which it works, the weight of the evidence indicates that homeownership for low-income households, when financed with manageable products, creates economic opportunity and contributes to an improved overall sense of control and satisfaction, even in the face of a severe economic downturn.

CAP as a Model in Troubled Times

The economic crisis offers lessons about the viability of community reinvestment lending in good times and bad. When we began our work, lenders and the secondary market lacked evidence about how loans to low- and moderate-income borrowers would perform. The CAP data fill that gap. Analysis of the CAP portfolio shows that affordable lending can be more resilient than other types of lending: the CAP portfolio performed well during the housing boom and continues (in terms of serious delinquency) to outperform all but fixed-rate prime mortgages following the economic decline.

The experiences of individual homeowners during the crisis show that promoting sustainable mortgages to lower income people can provide them with security both during economic booms and during economic downturns. Our findings suggest that any policy to promote sustainable lending to working families should be based on tried and true community reinvestment lending practices. The stress testing allowed by the onset of the crisis clearly demonstrates the viability of this type of lending. The CAP model shows how to create a more systemically stable mortgage market without stifling innovation, the kind of innovation that helps more Americans build long-term financial security. CAP's track record during the Great Recession indicates that there is good business to be done in underserved markets. Policymakers engaged in the debate about the desirability of promoting affordable homeownership should take notice. In the next chapter, we detail the lessons to be learned from comparing how CAP and subprime lenders approached these markets.

6 | *Ensuring Sustainable Homeownership*

We demonstrate in previous chapters that people with access to carefully designed mortgages do in fact experience what the Community Advantage Program was meant to accomplish: increased wealth, improved credit, and most important, sustained homeownership. We also examine some of the concrete benefits that homeownership provides to lower income families. Now we turn to the question of how these families can purchase a home—and remain in that home—as long as they want to. How can lower income people be given a chance to enjoy the same long-term benefits of homeownership—shelter, equity gains, and increased wealth—that higher income Americans now enjoy?

In this chapter, we glean lessons from our analysis in chapter 4. As we do so, we suggest changes to lending practice that will enable and extend homeownership to working families in a sustainable way moving forward. We recommend that lawmakers take four steps: restore sound product design, rein in careless underwriting, give originators appropriate incentives, and give loan servicers appropriate incentives.

Restore Sound Product Design

We base the stories of Tonya Hinton and Eddie and Laura Taylor on the experiences of the millions of low-income Americans who obtained mortgages during the housing boom, and their stories teach at least one clear lesson: mortgage design can either enable or thwart sustained homeownership. Eddie and Laura Taylor financed their home with a thirty-year, fixed-rate mortgage, the same type of product that has made homeownership accessible to so many Americans since the 1940s. In contrast, Tonya Hinton financed her home with a fee-laden, adjustable-rate mortgage, which she could afford only for the first few years, until its interest rate reset.

There is a clear difference between carefully underwriting mortgages with flexible guidelines and underwriting mortgages without regard to long-term sustainability. Our analysis of the over 46,000 affordable home loans in the CAP portfolio confirms that the thirty-year, fixed-rate mortgage is a safe, enduring product. CAP's serious delinquency rate is 7.6 percent, well below the 43 percent serious delinquency rate of subprime adjustable-rate borrowers across the United States and not much higher than the 5 percent serious delinquency rate of prime fixed-rate borrowers. Our research shows that product design matters: borrowers who hold subprime loans are about three to five times as likely to default as similar borrowers who obtained community reinvestment mortgages.

We also see how much risk is introduced by adjustable rates and exotic repayment features, compared with the standard, thirty-year, fixed-rate mortgage. At least part of this difference has to do with predictability. With a thirty-year, fixed-rate loan, a homeowner understands in advance what her monthly housing costs will be and can budget for predictable payments. Over the life of the loan, that payment gradually takes a relatively smaller piece of the borrower's monthly budget. With inflation, other costs increase, meaning the steady mortgage payment actually decreases in real dollars. A predictable mortgage payment makes the thirty-year, fixed-rate mortgage sustainable for many homeowners, but especially so for lower income families, which cannot tolerate sudden increases in their expenses. If underwritten properly, such loans allow low-income borrowers their best, and possibly only, opportunity for wealth building with a leveraged investment.

How does the thirty-year, fixed-rate loan benefit lenders? Financial institutions have over fifty years' experience originating this type of loan, which means that they can more easily evaluate any associated risks than they can with more exotic loan types. Lenders know that the thirty-year, fixed-rate loan has a record of predictable long-term performance, and its default rate is normally the lowest among home loan products. Concerned about inflation risks, lenders may be tempted to consider the appeal of adjustable-rate mortgages. However, over the years, secondary markets and rate hedging have evolved to effectively relieve rate risks.

What are the benefits of this product for investors? While the thirty-year, fixed-rate loan doesn't provide the high returns that more exotic subprime products promise, in the end exotic subprime loans do not necessarily provide those returns either. The thirty-year, fixed-rate loan does provide steady returns over the life of the loan. Consequently, it has proved a better long-term investment than many securities undergirded by subprime loans. For the sake of borrowers, lenders, and investors, then, the mortgage market must move "forward to the past," turning away from exotic products with their short-term outlook and returning to the durable, reliable, time-tested thirty-year, fixed-rate loan. The performance of this type of mortgage should form the basis for the future extension of credit in a sustainable manner.

However, markets are inherently innovative, and it is unlikely that lenders will restrict themselves to thirty-year, fixed-rate loans in the future. Because innovation will continue, consumers must be empowered with information that will let them choose carefully between different types of loans. Chapter 4 illustrates that Tonya Hinton, the borrower who eventually lost her home, didn't fully understand the terms of the mortgage she agreed to pay off. What hurt Tonya most was the fact that her mortgage came with a prepayment penalty about which she was unaware. In effect, this penalty meant that Tonya could not refinance into a loan she could afford before her interest rate reset.

Recent amendments to the Truth in Lending Act help address this problem. In October 2009 the Federal Reserve implemented new regulations requiring lenders to consider a borrower's ability to repay, based on verified income and assets and the highest scheduled payment in the first seven years of the loan. Prepayment penalties cannot last for more than two years for higher priced loans and are banned altogether for any mortgage if payments can change in the first four years. The new regulations also ban deceptive advertising practices, including referring to rates as "fixed" when they can in fact change. These amendments mean that borrowers like Tonya Hinton will not be priced out of refinancing into a more affordable product before their interest rates reset beyond their means. Additional rules are also set to be implemented to correct skewed incentives in the mortgage process. Originators will be prohibited from steering consumers to loans that are not in the borrowers' best interests. Yield spread premiums and certain other forms of originator compensation will be banned. Real estate appraisers will be prohibited from having financial or other interests in the properties or the lending transactions.

For consumers who want to take the additional step of ensuring they are working with a lender they can trust, a new nonprofit consumer education organization, the Fair Mortgage Collaborative (FMC), can help. Formed under the auspices of and with support from the Ford Foundation, the FMC creates and makes available online educational materials about many issues related to mortgage lending, including how to find a fair loan, how to identify and avoid predatory loans, whether you should use a broker and how to find one, and how to obtain good credit counseling services. FMC has taken the laudatory step of certifying—on request—those lenders who treat consumers fairly and who price their loans and services appropriately. Such voluntary certification will help consumers identify lenders who have a history of honest business practices.

Rein in Careless Underwriting

Our Tale of Two Borrowers also demonstrates that lenders must underwrite home loans with the specific goal of ensuring that borrowers can afford their mortgages over the long term. Yes, Eddie and Laura Taylor benefited from having access to a thirty-year, fixed-rate loan; however, they benefited even more because their lender screened them carefully to ensure that they could afford the monthly payments on their loan. Tonya's lender, on the other hand, didn't bother to assess whether or not she would be able to afford her mortgage after its interest rate reset.

In the mortgage underwriting process, a lender assesses whether it would be prudent to issue a home loan to a potential mortgagee. Underwriting determines whether the borrower can and will repay the loan. Underwriters focus on such factors as the borrower's income, how the mortgage payment compares to that income, the ratio between total debt and income, the borrower's credit history, and the borrower's assets, especially her savings. As we note in chapter 3, underwriters made several shifts in practice over the past decade that allowed more borrowers, and especially more low-income and minority borrowers, to become homeowners. The underwriting process allowed for alternative documentation of assets and income and permitted higher loan-to-value ratios. While we applaud innovation in each of these areas, we firmly believe that such innovation must be consistent with the goal of keeping people in their homes for the long term. Changes in underwriting practice must also remain consistent with the safe and sound operation of the institutions issuing home loans.

While underwriting used be an intensive, face-to-face process requiring reams of paperwork to verify an applicant's income and eligibility, over time it has relaxed somewhat. One case in point is the limited-documentation and no-documentation mortgages that lenders began making to self-employed individuals, whose income was not disbursed via a payroll system. Low-doc and no-doc mortgages were a helpful and sensible development in the lending system, since they allowed individuals with sufficient, though not documentable, income to become homeowners. By the height of the subprime mortgage bonanza, however, low-doc and no-doc loans, stated-income loans, and no-income/no-asset loans relaxed to the point of absurdity the documentation required to underwrite a mortgage.

Another problematic relaxation of underwriting that occurred during the subprime mortgage boom was the practice of underwriters qualifying borrowers for adjustable-rate mortgages based only on the loan's initial affordability. This is how Tonya Hinton got her mortgage. Hybrid subprime loans such as 2/28s and 3/27s started with a low fixed-rate for two or three years, followed by an adjustable rate for twenty-eight or twenty-seven years, respectively. Underwriters used only the low initial rate to evaluate the borrower's ability to afford the loan, even though the loan's interest rate would often reset beyond a point the owner could afford. This relaxation of underwriting standards defies common sense and good business practice.

Underwriters made a third change in procedure during the subprime bonanza: they increased the loan-to-value ratio for borrowers. Traditionally, a 20 percent down payment was the norm for obtaining a home loan; if borrowers put down less, lenders required mortgage insurance to mitigate default risk. More recently, however, borrowers were able to obtain financing for the full cost of their homes by using two mortgages, one for 80 percent of the value of the home and another for 20 percent. The share of subprime 80/20 purchase mortgage loans has been estimated as high as 50 percent in states with the greatest home price increases.[1] Although increasing the allowable loan-to-value ratio can be a viable way to enable lower income individuals to become homeowners (the CAP portfolio contains a number of mortgages issued for the full purchase price of the home), it should not be done without compensating factors. These factors can include the homebuyer undergoing prepurchase counseling or the homeowner holding a set amount of savings in reserve.

It should shock no one that underwriting changes that put borrowers into loans they could not afford triggered the mortgage crisis. The 2009 changes by the Federal Reserve to the Truth in Lending Act and the Home Ownership and Equity Protection Act rules prohibit lenders from making high-cost loans without considering the borrower's ability to repay the loan from their income and assets, which can no longer include the value of the home to be financed. Lenders must also assess a loan's affordability based on the highest scheduled payment in the first seven years of the loan. Finally, changes to the rules require lenders to verify the income and assets they rely upon to determine borrowers' ability to repay loans.

Our analysis of Community Advantage Program loans demonstrates that careful relaxation of underwriting practices can lead to sound and more widely accessible lending. Lenders should experiment with changing qualifying rules incrementally. Along the way, they should rigorously assess what works and what doesn't. This is what Self-Help, participating banks, and Fannie Mae did in the case of CAP. Lawmakers should ferret out and prohibit techniques that don't work, using as their criterion those that result in systemic default.

Give Originators Appropriate Incentives

Tonya Hinton and Eddie and Laura Taylor had very different experiences with their mortgages largely because of the way they obtained those mortgages. Our research shows that, controlling for creditworthiness of borrower, just who originates a loan is a major factor in determining whether the loan succeeds or fails. Specifically, we find that the higher default risk of subprime loans is significantly associated with the origination channel and with the characteristics of the product rather than with borrower characteristics.

Eddie and Laura Taylor obtained their mortgage from a mainstream bank through a program designed in accordance with the Community Reinvestment Act. The program required that the couple contribute savings toward their home's down payment and that they participate in a prepurchase homebuyer education program. Eddie and Laura's credit histories were thoroughly checked before the loan was issued, and the Taylors were required to keep one month's worth of principal, interest, taxes, and insurance funds in reserve. Their loan was a fixed-rate, thirty-year mortgage with no prepayment penalty and their interest rate was reasonable.

Tonya Hinton's loan, obtained through a mortgage broker, was for the full value of her home, required only limited documentation of her income, came with an exploding interest rate, and carried a hefty pre-payment penalty of which she was unaware. What could possibly have led Tonya's mortgage broker to issue a loan that she could not in fact afford and to attach to it penalties that essentially trapped her in the product?

At the time the borrowers in our tale were buying their houses, mortgage brokers across the United States were operating under a perverse set of incentives whereby they earned more when they steered borrowers into higher cost, riskier loans. Brokers who could convince borrowers to accept a loan with a higher interest rate earned a bonus payment called a yield spread premium. In some cases the unsuspecting borrower, who assumed the broker was working on his behalf, might not have been informed that he could in fact qualify for a lower interest rate.

Research by the Center for Community Capital adds to an emerging literature on the lending practices of mortgage brokers during the run-up in home prices before 2006. A steady decline in interest rates between mid-2000 and the end of 2003 created strong incentives for borrowers to refinance into lower rate mortgages. By the third wave of the CAP survey data collection in 2005, some 30 percent of these community reinvestment homeowners had refinanced into a new mortgage.

When we conducted the 2005 survey, we asked borrowers—among other things—whether they had refinanced. If so, we asked about both the refinancing process and the new mortgage product. Of the CAP borrowers who refinanced, 38 percent did so through a mortgage broker and 62 percent through a retail lender. We compared the experience of borrowers who refinanced through a broker with that of borrowers who refinanced through a bank. Specifically, we asked whether the lender initiated contact with the borrower, whether the terms of the mortgage changed at closing, and how satisfied the borrower felt in hindsight. We find that when borrowers refinanced with a mortgage broker rather than a retail lender, they had a less satisfactory refinancing process and were more likely to refinance into an adjustable-rate mortgage.

Clearly the practice of rewarding brokers for steering and locking their clients into high-cost, risky products is a disservice to homebuyers. We support moves to prohibit prepayment penalties on most home loans and to ban yield spread premiums based on varying loan terms such as higher interest rate. As we note above, changes to the Truth in Lending Act and the Home Ownership and Equity Protection Act do restrict and in some cases ban prepayment penalties; these restrictions are reinforced in the recently passed Dodd-Frank Wall Street Reform and Consumer Protection Act of 2010 (the Dodd-Frank Act, discussed at length in chapter 7). The same law addresses the problem of yield spread premiums.

Another way to ensure that brokers issue viable loans is to make their commission contingent on the performance of these loans. Tonya's broker originated her mortgage, passed it on to the lender, and then moved on to the next borrower. He earned his commission up front and kept his profit, even though Tonya later defaulted on the loan. Brokers must be held accountable for the viability of the loans they issue. They must have some "skin in the game" and must also have an incentive to issue loans that endure in the long term. One way to achieve both goals is to stop brokers from receiving all their commission up front. Brokers should earn their commission over a set time period from the stream of income generated by the loan. If the loan defaults, the commission stops at that point, before it is fully paid.

Give Loan Servicers Appropriate Incentives

The stories of Tonya Hinton and Eddie and Laura Taylor also show that servicing practices can make or break a successful entry into homeownership. When Eddie and Laura Taylor fell behind in their mortgage payments due to their daughter's medical expenses, their loan servicing agency took proactive steps to contact them early and negotiate a means by which they might catch up on their missed payments. While the couple did have to pay a late fee, they were current on their mortgage again within three months of the missed payment. The Taylors' experience is not uncommon: when low- and moderate-income homeowners who are behind on their mortgage payments participate in a repayment plan, they are 68 percent less likely to lose their homes.[2]

As we note earlier, when we analyze CAP's affordable home loans, we find that, after controlling for loan characteristics, borrower characteristics, and economic conditions, the likelihood that a delinquent borrower will default varies significantly across servicers. When low- and moderate-income borrowers fall behind in their mortgage payments, loan servicing practices can determine whether they will end up losing their homes through foreclosure.

Ironically, the only parties that proactive servicing does not benefit, at least as servicing is currently structured, are the loan servicers themselves. There is a shocking misalignment of incentives between servicers, on the one hand, and borrowers, lending institutions, and investors, on the other. Unlike other players in the lending process, the loan servicer does not normally lose money on a foreclosure and may even make money by charging fees during the foreclosure process. Affordable housing policy must address the fact that lenders, investors, and homeowners might benefit from curing a loan while servicers, who actually have the power to determine whether or not to foreclose, benefit from foreclosure. If servicers are to participate actively in keeping delinquent borrowers in their homes, they must be encouraged to be proactive about remedying delinquency and be discouraged from foreclosing. We suggest several ways to align servicer incentives with those of borrowers and lenders or investors.

First, servicers should not earn fees during the foreclosure process and perhaps should bear some of the costs of this process. This simple adjustment would help reduce the financial gain to be had from foreclosing quickly on borrowers.

Second, servicers should be able to earn a commission, or at least write down costs or taxes, when they help delinquent borrowers become and remain current on their home loans. The Home Affordable Modification Program (HAMP) offers compensation to reward servicers for helping owners remain in their homes. HAMP offers one-time and ongoing financial incentives to servicers for, among other things, modifying loans if those loans remain current for a set period of time and for reducing loan payments by a set percentage. Such incentives can help align the interests of servicers, borrowers, and lenders or investors.

Third, servicers should be rated on their performance, just as banks are rated under the Community Reinvestment Act. The servicer performance rating should center on how adept servicers are at keeping homeowners in their loans and thereby in their homes. Servicers with high ratings should be rewarded with a seal of approval that denotes to banks, investors, and the government-sponsored enterprises that the servicer works proactively to prevent loans from going into foreclosure. The seal of approval system would encourage servicers to work harder in the interests of homeowners, since banks, investors, and Fannie Mae and Freddie Mac would be unwilling to work with servicers with a history of poor loan performance.

In the meltdown of the private mortgage-backed securities market, contracts between investors and servicers, rules about tax-favored structures, and conflicts between investor classes all worked together to stop servicers from renegotiating with borrowers to avoid foreclosures. These contractual and legal barriers to taking steps that could benefit both borrowers and investors must be corrected.

Finally, consumers, who are the most directly affected by servicer practices, should be empowered to "vote with their feet." During the loan application process, potential borrowers should be able to select the servicer they want to work with. While servicer ratings and seals of approval could enable them to make a good choice, they should also have access to information about such things as the size of the company, staffing levels, expertise, and complaints filed against the servicer. This, more than anything else, would likely encourage servicers to change their business practices so that they are truly borrower focused.

The Community Advantage Program gives us a proven model upon which to base policy changes that ensure sound and equitable lending. We analyzed CAP's outcomes thoroughly, and the evidence shows clearly that CAP works from the standpoints of all concerned: borrowers, lenders, and investors. A question naturally follows from these findings: what would be required to bring CAP to scale nationally? In the next chapter, we answer this question.

7 | *Bringing Community Reinvestment Lending to Scale*

Throughout this book, we describe the elements that allowed low- and moderate-income families to enter into sustainable homeownership through the Community Advantage Program. In a narrow sense, this was achieved by providing borrowers with carefully underwritten, fixed-rate loans that they could afford to repay over time. The key to CAP's success, that is, the careful matching of affordable product with borrower, is documented in these pages and in the work of others.

But CAP's success would not have been possible without the broader mechanisms and structures that allowed the program to be created and then sustained over time. In this chapter, we describe these mechanisms and structures. We do so in order to consider how the CAP model might be brought to scale and provide homeownership opportunities for the millions of working families that are ready to realize this dream. We consider three things here: the credit enhancement mechanism that makes CAP work, the functions of the secondary market that allow the CAP program to thrive, and the broader systemic stability required for affordable home lending to take place.

A Credit Enhancement Mechanism

CAP succeeded in making billions of dollars of affordable loans available to low-income borrowers by filling the gap between primary depository lenders and the secondary market. The primary market lenders had the infrastructure, the branch presence, the motivation, and the community knowledge to provide safe mortgage loans to underserved markets, that is, those borrowers who could achieve homeownership without direct subsidies but who fell outside of traditional underwriting guidelines. What these lenders lacked was the necessary flow of capital to meet market needs efficiently. Fannie Mae and Freddie Mac, for their part, had access to capital but did not have the experience to serve this market well.

Self-Help stepped into this gap through the creation of CAP. Although Self-Help was a small, nonprofit financial institution, it had a powerful weapon at its disposal: a $50 million pool of capital made possible by a grant from the Ford Foundation. Instead of lending this money directly to borrowers, which would have tied up the funds for years to come, Self-Help used the $50 million to purchase over $4 billion in loans. It did so by using the $50 million as a credit enhancement that connected the capital resources of Fannie Mae to the primary origination network of the banks. Self-Help's ongoing liability for these loans enabled the sale of CAP loans in the secondary market. The credit enhancement allowed lenders to sell loans made to lower income borrowers in exchange for the capital to make new, similar loans.

CAP provides a proven model for connecting the primary and secondary markets in a way that both meets the needs of communities and encourages constructive innovation. By putting in place a similar mechanism to manage risks, a national credit enhancement fund could play a role like that of the Ford grant within CAP. Why is such a fund needed? Most important, it would serve to promote the safety and soundness of mortgage lending while ensuring that market participants continue to extend their services to all qualified borrowers. To better achieve these goals—that is, sustainable lending to a broad population—a special insurance fund would provide the needed credit enhancement. The fund would be used to manage the risks of affordable, fixed-rate loans that are originated and securitized nationally.

As in all policy recommendations, we come swiftly to the matter of cost: just who would pay for this credit enhancement fund? The market is a continuum wherein the stability of one segment is dependent upon the stability of the whole spectrum; we have clear evidence of this from the recent subprime lending fiasco. Since all industry benefits from systemic stability, then all industry should contribute to achieving the same.

We contend that in the aftermath of the Great Recession, community reinvestment lending efforts such as CAP must be brought to scale if the country is to minimize systemic risks and ensure access to credit for lower income homeowners. Private sector capital, sustainable innovation, and careful oversight are all hallmarks of CAP, and they should be hallmarks of lending to lower income people moving forward. However, bringing the CAP program to scale requires the existence of a well-functioning secondary market within which affordable home loans can be sold. Further, it requires systemic stability throughout the financial sector. We examine these issues in the next two sections.

Beyond the Primary Lenders: Secondary-Market Functions That Enable CAP

CAP could not have succeeded in making over $4 billion available to lower income homeowners without the participation of Fannie Mae in purchasing these loans, and so the question of bringing CAP to scale necessarily raises the question of the secondary market's future. Here we do not focus on the actual structure of the secondary market moving forward but on what crucial functions the secondary market has played, and must continue to play, in the provision of housing finance for America's working families.

Until the recent housing market collapse, the U.S. housing finance system was considered a model to be imitated. In large part, this was due to the level of maturity achieved in the traditional primary sector of the market. It was the development of a regulated secondary market that enabled that maturity. By pooling and managing risk, the secondary-market system ensured the smooth functioning of the U.S. housing finance system. The means for doing so evolved and were refined over time but in the end led to the efficient commoditization of mortgages. Government-sponsored enterprises—Fannie Mae and Freddie Mac—evolved to fill this function. Unfortunately, with the onset of the Great Recession, it became obvious that the finance system had not achieved the same level of maturity throughout.

Criticisms of the structure of the GSEs (that is, their public-private nature) and of their role in the housing finance crisis should be differentiated from a discussion of the necessary role these institutions play in enabling the smooth working of the U.S. mortgage markets and economy. Whatever is done with the GSEs themselves, there is a need to put in place mechanisms to safeguard the following benefits that in the past the GSEs provided to the housing finance system: the promotion of liquidity, the cross-subsidization of risk, the standardization of mortgage products, the promotion of affordability, and the generation of new products and risk management strategies.

First and foremost, the goal of a properly functioning secondary market is the promotion of liquidity. Liquidity in the housing finance system is created when loans are purchased from lenders in exchange for capital that lenders can use to make additional loans. The GSEs promoted liquidity in the housing finance system by purchasing loans from banks; some of these were held in the GSEs' portfolios, while others were bundled into mortgage-backed securities and sold to investors, thereby giving the GSEs additional funds with which to purchase more loans). Mortgage-backed securities can be bought and sold many times in a day; in contrast, it may take investors four to eight weeks to sell an individual whole loan. The securitization process facilitated the promotion of liquidity and attracted trillions of dollars from around the globe into the U.S. home mortgage market. While the private sector can perform this function in good times, it cannot do so throughout the full business cycle. This suggests that there is a need for public sector involvement in the purchasing of loans and the creation of mortgage-backed securities.

A secondary market also enables lenders to manage and spread risks related to local economic conditions. For instance, when a regional economy is challenged, a local lender may be too weak and risk averse to make mortgages in that market, even to the best bor-

Fannie Mae and Freddie Mac:
The Good, the Bad, and the (Not So) Ugly

There is heated debate over the role of Fannie Mae and Freddie Mac in the housing market's collapse, and we pause here to examine their complex role in the crisis. We do so to help the reader distinguish between the positive contributions of these government-sponsored enterprises (GSEs) from their reckless behavior during the housing bubble and also from their more recent activity under conservatorship.

The Good

In the aftermath of the savings and loans crisis in the late 1980s, Fannie Mae and Freddie Mac came to dominate the mortgage market. Between 1993 and 2003, the GSEs, including their mortgage pools, accounted for more than half of all home mortgage debt outstanding, even as the total amount of that debt more than doubled to over $7 trillion.[a] In the process, the GSEs delivered a commoditized, efficiently priced mortgage product that helped sustain the American middle class. The vast majority of these loans were prime mortgages: for example, two-thirds of all single-family mortgages purchased by Fannie Mae and Freddie Mac between 2001 and 2003 were fixed-rate mortgages, with loan-to-value (LTV) ratios no greater than 80 percent, and issued to borrowers with credit scores of at least 660.[b]

The GSEs also purchased some less conservative mortgages, in part to satisfy their public mission. These mortgages included loans with LTVs over 90 percent or to borrowers with credit scores under 620. However, these loans often had credit enhancements to protect the agencies against losses. In fact, Fannie Mae and Freddie Mac are prohibited by their charter from buying loans with LTV ratios above 80 percent unless other parties, most commonly private mortgage insurance companies, bear the risk. Between 2001 and 2003, Fannie Mae and Freddie Mac purchased nearly $500 billion in mortgages with either or both features (LTV ratio > 90, credit score < 620) accounting for 69 percent of all such loans.

But portfolio caps and the growth of private label securities limited Fannie Mae and Freddie Mac's further exposure. Between 2004 and 2006, at the peak of the housing bubble, their purchase of low credit score or high LTV loans fell to $342 billion, which accounted for less than 40 percent of all such loans. Further, these loans never accounted for more than 15 percent of Fannie Mae and Freddie Mac's overall purchases in a year. In comparison, 40 percent of mortgages packaged into private label securities between 2001 and 2006 were either low credit score or high LTV. Moreover, the vast majority (nearly 90 percent) of such loans purchased by Fannie Mae and Freddie Mac were fixed-rate mortgages, compared to just 23 percent of similar mortgages financed by the private market.

Our research shows that product features, such as adjustable rates and prepayment penalties, can add significantly to the chances of default.[c] Traditional mortgage products help explain why the ninety-day-plus delinquency rate for Fannie Mae's mortgages to borrowers with credit scores under 620 peaked at 18.2 percent at the end of 2009, while the delinquency rate for market subprime loans reached over 30 percent.[d]

The Bad

Where Fannie Mae and Freddie Mac abandoned their practice of supporting the issuance of traditional mortgages, they suffered substantial losses.

Alt-A loans generally involve higher loan balances, higher credit scores, and low documentation of income and assets. As such, they are unlikely to satisfy the GSE's affordable housing goals. Nevertheless, Fannie Mae and Freddie Mac steadily increased their purchases of these loans, blurring the valuable distinction between agency prime and nonagency subprime.[e] As a result, they are suffering high default rates on these loans. Fannie Mae reports that Alt-A loans account for just 8 percent of its single-family book of business but over 35 percent of its credit losses over the past several years.[f]

In addition, Fannie Mae and Freddie Mac began purchasing private label securities; these purchases increased from $5.7 billion in 1997 to $221.3 billion in 2005. Inverting the established mortgage finance system, this business fed Fannie Mae and Freddie Mac's competitors and transferred market share to less regulated market players with poor underwriting standards. The agencies generally limited themselves to the supposedly lower risk senior tranches of

(continued)

mortgage-backed securities. As of the second quarter of 2007, over 90 percent of Fannie Mae's private label mortgage-backed securities were rated AAA by Standard & Poor's and Moody's. Unfortunately, these securities were drastically overrated. Between 2008 and 2009, Moody's downgraded 80 percent of the tranches it originally rated AAA. Mark-to-market policies required Fannie Mae and Freddie Mac to reduce the reported value of their investments, causing massive losses. Fannie Mae and Freddie Mac's capital markets segments, which include purchases of mortgage-backed securities, combined for a loss of over $57 billion in 2008 alone, accounting for over half of net losses that year.[g] The GSEs were unprepared to sustain such losses.

The (Not So) Ugly

Fannie Mae and Freddie Mac's insolvency was triggered by a combination of undercapitalization and downgrades in their investments. They were forced into conservatorship in September 2008. Since then they have operated as an arm of the federal government to help stabilize the housing market and banking sector. As the private label market evaporated, Fannie Mae and Freddie Mac, in addition to the Federal Housing Administration, have become the only outlets for new mortgage finance. The agencies have been a vehicle to modify and refinance high LTV and otherwise distressed mortgages to prevent more foreclosures. Since this might entail future losses, it is an effort that private market actors would not be willing, and cannot be expected, to take on.

Not surprisingly, the potential costs to taxpayers could be staggering, in the hundreds of billions of dollars. Ultimately, the final accounting for the rescue of Fannie Mae and Freddie Mac won't be done for some time. Over time, profits from the post-2008 business will offset some of the taxpayers' support. Two other factors will affect the total cost of rescuing these agencies, both outside of the control of the GSEs: the path of the economy and what the government decides to do with the secondary mortgage market. Harder to quantify are the immeasurable benefits realized through the rescue of the GSEs. Some of these can be measured: the dividend they pay to taxpayers, the subsidy to the banks from absorbing losses the banks should have taken, and the benefits to investors from making good on guarantees. However, the biggest benefit, that of stabilizing and strengthening the housing market and the financial sector, will be impossible to quantify.

    a. Board of Governors of the Federal Reserve System, "Federal Reserve Statistical Release, Z.1, Flow of Funds Accounts of the United States," March 2010.

    b. Federal Housing Finance Agency, "Data on the Risk Characteristics and Performance of Single-Family Mortgages Originated from 2001 through 2008 and Financed in the Secondary Market" (2010) (www.fhfa.gov/Default.aspx?Page=313).

    c. Lei Ding and others, "Risky Borrowers or Risky Mortgages: Disaggregating Effects Using Propensity Score Models" (Center for Community Capital, University of North Carolina, 2010).

    d. Fannie Mae, "2009 Credit Supplement" (2010) (www.fanniemae.com/media/pdf/newsreleases/2009_10K_credit_summary.pdf); Mortgage Bankers Association, *National Delinquency Survey* (2009) (Moody's Analytics' Databuffet.com).

    e. Kevin Park, "Understanding Capital: Fannie, Freddie, and the Foreclosure Crisis" (2010) (www.ccc.unc.edu/documents/FannieFreddieForeclosure.pdf).

    f. Fannie Mae, "2010 Third-Quarter Credit Supplement" (www.fanniemae.com/ir/pdf/sec/2010/q3credit_summary.pdf).

    g. Park, "Understanding Capital."

rowers. In contrast, a lender that can pool risks nationally can continue to lend in all markets, without raising rates in weaker local markets, because it can pool loans across markets. Local markets can go through many cycles in the life of a typical mortgage; loans made in today's weak markets may in future years be subsidizing loans made in other markets. Just as risks can be managed across regions, they can also be pooled across property types, borrower characteristics, and time periods. The pooling of risk is a crucial secondary-market function and makes for a more stable and efficient housing finance system.

The standardization of mortgage products is another purpose of well-functioning secondary markets. In the U.S. market, standardization is built on the foundation of the amortizing fixed-rate mortgage. As discussed throughout this book, these mortgages are the safest and most sustainable form of home lending. Unfortunately, depository institutions are understandably reluctant to assume the interest rate risks associated with fixed-rate mortgages and prefer adjustable-rate instruments, which shift interest rate risk to borrowers. It is only because lenders have been able to sell fixed-rate mortgages in the secondary market that banks have been willing to originate fixed-rate loans. The standardization of mortgage products in the United States led to the development of the TBA market (shorthand for "to be announced"), which allows borrowers to lock a mortgage rate thirty, sixty, or ninety days in advance of closing. This is possible only because standardization allows all parties involved to feel comfortable committing funds even before loans are actually originated.

Another crucial function of the secondary market in the United States has been the promotion of affordability for borrowers. Affordability stems in part from the sharing of risk and the standardization of mortgage products. It has also been enhanced by the development of different types of mortgage originators, such as mortgage brokers and bankers who originate loans and sell them in the secondary market. Because these entities do not require significant capital for their operations, they can compete aggressively for business with each other and with traditional banks, leading to lower costs for borrowers.

Finally, a stable secondary market must have the capacity to fund loans that cannot be easily packaged into securities. For example, the GSEs purchased and held in portfolio a significant number of nonstandard multifamily loans on properties financed with low-income housing tax credits. They also used their portfolios to pilot new products and eventually produced securities backed by nontraditional mortgages after a period of experimentation. Their ability to hold loans in portfolio and experiment with different ways of managing risk, including the flexibility to work out problems with borrowers who fall behind on their mortgage payments, is an important function of the secondary market: private entities are unlikely to enter markets where risks are unknown, and if they did it would likely lead to unsustainable practices.

What will the housing finance system look like if these secondary-market functions are not maintained? First, current trends of credit tightening and market segmentation are likely to continue. The pricing of risks on the basis of specific borrower, loan, and property characteristics may be an attractive management tool, but it is likely to exacerbate market stratification to the point where nonprime borrowers have ever more undesirable (and riskier) credit options.

Second, increased volatility is likely to happen in various segments of the market. Traditionally, housing and housing finance markets were considered to be countercyclical: when the overall economy weakened, housing markets provided a relatively safe haven for investors. The increasing integration of mortgage markets into capital markets has made residential markets more volatile. Unfortunately, volatility seems greater in the less developed sectors, that is, the nonprime market. In the absence of a mature credit market for nonprime borrowers, volatility will make it even more difficult for working families to obtain a sustainable fixed-rate product at a reasonable price.

In sum, broadly speaking, bringing to scale community reinvestment efforts such as CAP requires all of the secondary-market functions described in this section. Can or would fully private secondary-market institutions fulfill these functions in a manner that provides long-term stability? It is possible to envision private entities doing so at the high end of the market or when times are good. However, it is difficult to envision that they will do so in a stable and sustainable manner at all times and for all segments of the market. Faced with the inability of private institutions to deliver these functions consistently and broadly, one or more public purpose entities with some form of government support may be needed.

Obviously, a well-functioning secondary market needs to be part of a broader stable economic system. In July 2010 President Obama signed into law the Dodd-Frank Wall Street Reform and Consumer Protection Act (the Dodd-Frank Act), taking a major step forward toward the maintenance of systemic stability. It is to this topic that we now turn.

Systemic Stability: The Dodd-Frank Act

The 848-page Dodd-Frank Act aims at comprehensive reform of the financial regulatory system in an effort to stave off another near collapse of U.S. financial markets. In the words of the act, its goals are "to promote the financial stability of the United States by improving accountability and transparency in the financial system, to end 'too big to fail,' to protect the American taxpayer by ending bailouts, [and] to protect consumers from abusive financial services practices."[1] The actual workings of the law will be sorted out in political wrangling, so we present here only an overview of the act's basic elements.[2]

The Dodd-Frank Act establishes the Financial Stability Oversight Council, composed of ten federal financial regulators, one independent member, and five nonvoting members; the council is chaired by the treasury secretary. The council is tasked with identifying "risks to the financial stability of the United States that could arise from the material financial distress or failure, or ongoing activities, of large, interconnected bank holding companies or nonbank financial companies, or that could arise outside the financial services marketplace." As part of its mission, the council must determine which institutions are large enough to pose a systemic threat. The council must decide how to respond to such a threat: the law empowers the council to impose restrictions on large, troubled financial firms and creates a process by which the government might dismantle such companies at no cost to taxpayers.

Another goal of the Dodd-Frank Act is to enhance consumer protection via establishment of the Consumer Financial Protection Bureau, housed within the Federal Reserve. The bureau is established to "ensure American consumers get the clear, accurate information they need to shop for mortgages, credit cards, and other financial products, and protect them from hidden fees, abusive terms, and deceptive practices."[3] The bureau is empowered under the act to promulgate mortgage underwriting standards that ban deceptive and abusive lending practices. It has responsibility for overseeing other consumer-related statutes, including the Home Mortgage Disclosure Act and recent credit card reform legislation.

The Dodd-Frank Act also aims to regulate banks' trading activities by requiring overseers to "implement regulations for banks, their affiliates and holding companies, to prohibit proprietary trading, investment in and sponsorship of hedge funds and private equity funds, and to limit relationships with hedge funds and private equity funds." As part of the new restrictions, the act prohibits banks whose deposits are federally insured from trading for their own benefit, though banks are still allowed to earn profits that are incidental to the trades they engage in. Since the goal of making a profit underlies all financial transactions, it will be difficult for both regulators and regulated banks to parse out which profits are intentional and which are incidental to trading activities.

Further, the act tasks the Commodity Futures Trading Commission (CFTC) and the Securities and Exchange Commission (SEC) with carrying out new regulations concerning derivatives. The act aims to create transparency in the exchange of derivatives and does so by requiring that most swaps be cleared and traded on an exchange, rather than privately. The act also requires the collection and publication of data concerning derivatives exchanges. Those engaging in the exchange of derivatives are required to have "adequate financial resources to meet responsibilities," and the CFTC and SEC are granted the authority to regulate derivatives so that "irresponsible practices and excessive risk-taking can no longer escape regulatory oversight."

How does the Dodd-Frank Act address the practices that led to the mortgage crisis? First, it requires that lenders ensure each borrower's ability to repay the loan before issuing the loan. Second, it prohibits the financial incentives that led to the proliferation of subprime lending, banning yield spread premiums and curtailing the use of prepayment penalties. Third, the act broadens the definition of who is protected under federal law by lowering the interest rate, points, and fees that define high-cost loans; further, it requires escrows of taxes and insurance for high-cost loans. Fourth, the law requires lenders to qualify borrowers based on the fully indexed rate for adjustable-rate mortgages, requires lenders to disclose the maximum a consumer would pay on an adjustable-rate mortgage, and requires lenders to warn consumers that payments on adjustable-rate mortgages will vary with interest rate changes. Fifth, the law designates that qualified mortgages may have origination fees no higher than 3 percent, must be fully documented, may have a term no longer than thirty years, and may not be negatively amortizing or interest-only loans. Finally, the act establishes penalties for noncompliance with the law, including fees as high as three years' worth of interest payments as well as damages; borrowers who have been victims of a violation of the new standards may not be foreclosed upon. The law bans mandatory arbitration clauses from home loans.[4]

As important and ambitious as it is, the Dodd-Frank Act is just one necessary component in promoting the stability of a financial system within which community reinvestment efforts such as CAP might thrive. The challenge that policymakers face is to identify and reinforce the fundamental elements of the overall financial system that will increase stability and access in all segments of the housing finance system. We turn to this issue in the next chapter.

8 | *Regaining the Dream*

It is difficult to envision a stable future in the middle of a crisis. Yet the only way out of the crisis is to identify and reinforce the elements of the financial system that will increase stability and access in the housing finance market. In chapter 7 we describe the ways in which community reinvestment efforts such as CAP might be brought to scale, including the creation of a national credit enhancement mechanism, the need for supportive secondary-market functions, and the maintenance of systemic stability.

Now we turn to the core elements of a housing finance policy that will enable community reinvestment lending, and indeed all sound mortgage lending, going forward. To be effective, housing finance and regulatory policy must promote well-functioning markets, encourage the appropriate use of technological innovation, align the interests of market participants, minimize potential conflicts of interest, and guarantee the well-being of consumers in the mortgage marketplace. We consider each of these in turn.

Promote Well-Functioning Markets

The Great Recession, as the crisis that started in late 2006 has come to be known, made it painfully clear that financial markets do not regulate themselves. Leading up to and ultimately causing the crisis, market participants raced to the bottom, seeking short-term gains and ignoring long-term consequences. These participants were responding rationally to a range of short-term economic incentives, but the collective impact of their behavior led to an economic catastrophe. The financial market's failure to self-regulate provides a strong justification for more, and more effective, government regulation.

Not everyone interprets recent events in this way. A "government is the problem" mantra has increasingly ruled the public policy debate since the late 1970s, and there are those who argue that reduced government intervention in America's financial and housing markets is the only way to strengthen these markets. This thinking ignores the fact, of course, that neither market would exist were it not for the government creating and nurturing them to maturity, a point clearly illustrated in our description of the evolution of the housing finance system in chapter 2.

Some argue that the government's involvement in the housing and financial markets should have been restricted to the creation of these markets. Advocates for privatization believe that U.S. financial and housing markets are able to operate efficiently, now that they are mature, and that the various activities of each market are best left to the private sector. We respectfully disagree with these assertions.

Not all activities undertaken by governments are ideal for privatization. There are activities that the private sector can take on profitably after the public sector has created a market for them, but there are other activities that require continued public sector participation because they are not viable or profitable without such involvement. The provision of affordable housing to lower income working families is one such example. While this activity can be profitable, it may not be profitable enough relative to other investment opportunities to attract the capital necessary to fund it. The government has a crucial role to play in ensuring the flow of credit to families that are willing to work for homeownership and that simply need a fair opportunity to achieve this goal.

Obviously, policymakers must ensure that regulation does not stifle the enormous economic benefits that result from the operation of a healthy and innovative financial sector. Ideally, this sector promotes economic growth, allocates capital to where it is most needed, and manages risks broadly across the whole system. Only a financial sector that is robust can resist economic shocks. Effective regulation is an essential element in the development and maintenance of a thriving financial sector.[1]

In *Politics and Banking*, Susan Hoffmann states that "a regulatory framework institutionalizes a way of thinking about the public world."[2] To regulate markets effectively, we first need to identify the public objectives we are trying to achieve. In the aftermath of the housing finance crisis, these objectives should include financial stability through the promotion of broad and constant market liquidity, systemic stability achieved through stakeholder protection and responsible risk oversight, and wide and fair availability of affordable mortgage credit.

With regard to financial stability and liquidity, while policymakers cannot prevent financial shocks, they can work to mitigate their effects by enhancing the overall soundness of individual institutions and their practices. Ideally, regulators accomplish this goal through their supervisory role. More narrowly, regulators can ensure that institutions that form the core of the financial system manage the risks that they face in a safe and sound manner.[3] As recent history shows, this is difficult to achieve in the presence of large financial conglomerates formed by a complex array of affiliates and subsidiaries, many of them outside regulatory oversight. Although it is unclear how it will ultimately work in practice, it is heartening that the Dodd-Frank Act aims to discourage the desire of institutions to grow in size and complexity to the point where they become too big to fail—and equally heartening that regulators are empowered to liquidate troubled institutions that in fact pose such a risk.

Stakeholder protection is another vital public objective. The stability of the system is undermined when investors and consumers lose confidence in it. Of course, the goal of effective regulation should not be to prevent stakeholder losses: for markets to work properly, stakeholders must be allowed to bear the consequences of their decisions.

However, stakeholders are entitled to the information necessary to make decisions appropriate to their personal financial circumstances. Effective policy can contribute to market integrity by enhancing stakeholder protections and making sure everybody involved understands and adheres to the rules of the game.[4] It is equally important to prevent insider trading and market manipulation. Regulators must stamp out the possibility of regulatory arbitrage, whereby market participants shop around for the most lenient regulator or seek out unregulated areas in the hope of gaining market share. Regulators must also prevent misinformation, manipulation of information, and other activities that lead to unsustainable lending and undermine public confidence.

Finally, effective policy needs to encourage the wide and fair availability of affordable mortgage credit. Some argue that properly functioning free markets will lead to this outcome—that is, that the solution to the mortgage lending crisis is not more but less regulation. We contest this view. We agree with Dan Immergluck that progress in achieving access to affordable, sound credit has "involved a strong, proactive role for the public sector, both in providing and standardizing mortgage credit and in providing a regulatory infrastructure that constrains market booms and busts."[5] In both of these capacities, the government must remain active. As we demonstrate in chapter 2, market failure and past government action led over many decades to patterns of lending that resulted in the limited availability of prime credit in many minority and low-income communities. Effective market regulation needs to address the possibility that market failure might lead to and exacerbate inequality, especially in the aftermath of the financial crisis.

Tame the Darker Side of Technological Innovation

As is often the case with innovation, technological advances have been both beneficial and detrimental to housing finance markets. On the one hand, credit scoring models and automated underwriting reduce the time and cost required to underwrite and originate mortgages and allow the market to charge individual borrowers the estimated true cost of borrowing. This made credit available to some who could not have obtained it previously. On the other hand, the same tools allowed institutions to steer borrowers to expensive mortgages that were highly profitable for the lender, at least in the short term. Ultimately, this led to market segmentation, specialization, and the meteoric rise of subprime lending.

Should the lending industry price loans according to the risk factors of a given borrower, loan, and property just because technology makes this possible? We don't think so, and we support this assertion with an example from the health insurance industry. Ideally, health insurance companies need to insure young, healthier individuals so they can provide coverage to older, more illness-prone people at a reasonable cost. The system can only work if risks are pooled. A company that sells insurance only to unhealthy individuals would have to either charge exorbitant premiums to cover the greater risk of illness among this population or go bankrupt. Faced with high premiums, unhealthy individuals would be less likely to have coverage, would avoid routine medical care, and would eventually need costlier care, worsening their risk profile.

Managing the risks of mortgage lending can be understood in a similar way. When large numbers of mortgages are pooled, the attendant risks are spread. With mortgages, as with health insurance, most participants are low risk. Blending everyone's risk covers those who are high risk and increases only very slightly the cost for those who are low risk. Meanwhile, the higher risk participants in the pool get access to a quality loan product at a price that mitigates their risk of default.

Of course, none of this means that mortgage credit should be made available to all: many are not ready to assume the long-term responsibilities of homeownership. However, technology helped to create a false line between those with access to the prime market and those excluded from it. The lenders involved in the Community Advantage Program model one way to bridge that gap. CAP loans were made after careful consideration and documentation of borrowers' individual financial circumstances. Through the use of thoughtful underwriting, lenders can more ably distinguish which borrowers are creditworthy.

Align the Interests of Market Participants

A stable and sustainable housing finance system requires a basic alignment of interests among market participants. In the absence of this, one participant can create a moral hazard by passing risk on to others. For example, a primary lender might sell its worst loans to the secondary market and might keep all of its best loans in portfolio. From a broad perspective, alignment of interests will minimize the likelihood that market participants will act in ways that contribute to systemic failure.

A simple way to achieve an alignment of interests among participants is to require that all parties involved in the lending process retain some degree of liability. From loan originators to issuers of mortgage-backed securities, everybody should be required to retain some stake in how each loan ultimately performs. The Dodd-Frank Act recognizes this: it attempts to increase the accountability of those issuing mortgage-backed securities by requiring that issuers retain at least 5 percent of the associated credit risk (unless the underlying loans meet standards that reduce riskiness).

How might a similar process work for banks? A lending institution could withhold 10 percent of the commission paid to loan officers until the quality of the business they originate is known. After some period of time, the institution could pay the rest of the commission depending on the extent of early payment defaults, past dues, and charge-offs. To our knowledge, only one lending institution—North Carolina-based BB&T—has such an arrangement in place.[6]

Similarly, mortgage bankers who originate products and sell them could be required to set aside reserve funds against default. The investors would return the reserve funds to the mortgage banker once enough time had passed to reveal how well the loans were performing. In the finance industry, this is referred to as "funded indemnification."[7] Requiring those who sell mortgage-backed securities to set aside a percentage against risk, as Self-Help did with Fannie Mae, achieves the same goal.

Bearing the risk associated with any investment is not, in itself, enough; risks must also be backed by real capital. To align the interests of the various parties in the lending process, all institutions must be subject to similar rules concerning capital requirements. Before the crisis, this was not the case; different kinds of financial institutions were required to meet different capital and leverage ratios.[8] This gave rise to regulatory arbitrage and rewarded those institutions that had the least capital at stake. If all participants retain partial liability, however, capital requirements can be more consistent across institutions.

Minimize Potential Conflicts of Interest

A stable and sustainable housing finance system also requires minimizing conflicts of interest, especially in the arena of credit ratings. At one time ratings agencies charged investors for making such assessments. Unfortunately, that changed in the 1970s, when the ratings agencies instead started charging fees to bond issuers. They were paid by the very firms that sold the rated securities to investors. Obviously, this created a conflict of interest because the agencies had the incentive to serve the bond issuers rather than the investors. In practice, if a ratings agency gave a less favorable rating to a security, the issuer of that security would be likely to avoid future business with that agency.

The Dodd-Frank Act includes provisions that attempt to address conflicts of interest for the credit rating agencies. The act creates an Office of Credit Ratings, housed within the Securities and Exchange Commission. This office will examine each "nationally recognized statistical ratings organization" (NRSRO) once a year and make public its findings. The act also attempts to address the "revolving door" issue between the ratings agencies and their clients by requiring that ratings agencies report to the SEC when certain officers associated with the NRSRO leave to work for companies for which ratings have been issued within the past twelve months. Further, the act includes provisions that will prevent issuers of asset-backed securities from shopping for the agency that will give them the highest rating.

As far as these provisions go, policymakers must be sure to address the potential conflict of interest created by the credit rating agencies' business model, wherein they are paid by the very parties whose profit depends on the ratings. The credit rating agencies played a key role in making mortgage-backed securities and collateralized debt obligations attractive to institutional investors and to the government-sponsored enterprises. They did so by issuing excessively optimistic assessments of subprime mortgages and related securities. Policymakers can address this situation in several ways, including requiring the agencies to work for investors again. Another option is for a clearinghouse to match ratings agencies to security issuers on a semi-random basis; under this system, the agencies would feel less pressure to give a favorable rating out of fear of losing future business. Alternatively, federal regulators could develop their own standards of creditworthiness to be used industry-wide, instead of relying solely on the assessments from ratings agencies.

Expand Consumer Rights and Protections

Finally, a stable and sustainable housing finance system requires strong consumer protections. Ensuring that consumers have access to safe and sound products and full information regarding the workings of these products is the purview of the new Consumer Financial Protection Bureau (CFPB), established under the Dodd-Frank Act. For the most part, the CFPB is narrowly empowered to inform the public and ban deceptive and abusive lending practices, thus leading to more sustainable credit options. In this section, we offer suggestions about additional means for enhancing consumer protections.

For regulation to be effective, consumers must have more power in the mortgage lending process. The past decade shows that the effectiveness of regulatory oversight may shift with the political winds. Even if effective regulation is in place, philosophical opposition and other factors may cause the regulators of the moment to opt for lax enforcement. To some extent, consumers empowered with more information and the right to legal redress can withstand these changing political winds. Moreover, increasing consumer protections can compensate when regulation adapts too slowly to rapid change in the mortgage market.

Policymakers have addressed consumer protection at the individual level largely by creating disclosure rules. Unfortunately, as the recent past shows, the information disclosed has not protected consumers adequately against risky loan terms nor shielded investors against the risks inherent in securities composed of unsustainable loans. To a large extent, consumers were inadequately informed about true long-term costs because the coverage of the 1994 Home Ownership and Equity Protection Act (HOEPA) was limited. The law aimed to provide consumer protection against the worst predatory loan terms, but in reality it applied to fewer than 1 percent of all loans and so protected very few borrowers.[9]

The Federal Reserve revised HOEPA regulations to ban unfair, deceptive, and abusive mortgage practices—but only in July 2008, after the onset of the crisis. At that point, it banned egregious practices that in retrospect appear blatantly reckless: originating higher cost loans without regard to a borrower's ability to repay, coercing appraisers to misstate or misrepresent a dwelling's value, and including prepayment penalties in loans where payments can change within four years of origination. Though late, these changes are welcome. The requirements of the Dodd-Frank Act expand these restrictions.

However, we believe that consumer rights should also include easy access to information about the quality of loan servicers. Complaints about originators, lenders, and servicers should be centralized so that consumers can look for systematic patterns of poor service. A promising model is the recently formed Fair Mortgage Collaborative, which we describe in chapter 6. This nonprofit organization educates consumers about predatory lending practices, helps them avoid predatory lenders and brokers, and enables them to obtain safe, fairly priced loans.

At the community level, the Community Reinvestment Act provides a good example of regulation from the consumer perspective. Making community reinvestment lending evaluations public provides consumers with information about an institution's lending practices. Consumer advocates can then challenge a bank's investment activities when that bank wants to expand. The Home Mortgage Disclosure Act provides affordable housing and fair lending advocates with the data they need to assess for and litigate against the disparate treatment of borrowers or the disparate impact of seemingly neutral policies.

But we believe that a rigorous evaluation of the practices of lending institutions should not be left only to activists, academics, and lawyers. In the years just before the crisis, the federal agencies that assessed for Community Reinvestment Act compliance should have ascertained whether the institutions they were evaluating engaged in risky practices, such as originating loans without regard to a borrower's long-term ability to pay. Instead, CRA does not generally distinguish qualitatively between high-cost lending and prime lending (except for the requirements for safety and soundness). Moreover, CRA allows regulators to ignore the activities of affiliates, which could be making high-cost mortgages right in the banks' assessment areas. Further, we should recognize that many of the various functions required to create, fund, and service mortgages are performed somewhere in the domain of CRA-covered institutions. For example, there is no scrutiny of how the mortgage-servicing function is helping to meet the credit needs of the target communities. We contend that more CRA-relevant activities should be evaluated going forward, and all of this information should be made available to the public.

Finally, bankruptcy reform must enhance consumer protection. Under current law, borrowers can modify all types of debt in bankruptcy court—all, that is, except the mortgage on their primary residence. Borrowers cannot have their mortgage debt reduced as an alternative to foreclosure, even if the loan was inappropriately underwritten. This limitation of the law puts consumers at a disadvantage when lenders offer a mortgage without considering its long-term sustainability. This is unfair, and it must change.

Looking Ahead

As difficult as it is to predict the future, we can visualize two alternatives. One outcome adapts the lessons learned and the evidence collected from both successes and failures. The other disregards the evidence and will lead the country to repeat its mistakes.

In these pages, we identify a number of key factors that characterize a stable, post-crisis housing finance system. These factors include everything from underwriting that leads to sustainable lending at the primary level to the alignment of incentives among capital market institutions.

Commonsense underwriting should characterize mortgage lending moving forward. Our research convinces us that appropriately underwritten fixed-rate mortgages, even with low down payments, are sustainable and provide an opportunity for wealth building for families that lack other investment opportunities. We also know that these loans can be made in a manner that is profitable for capital market investors.

That said, homeownership is not the antidote for all ills, including an individual's financial insecurity. The belief that homeownership is suitable for everyone was a pre-crisis misconception that should not drive future policy. Homeownership is not for everybody: many people are not yet ready to assume the responsibilities that come with purchasing a home due to life cycle, employment, or financial considerations. Others may never be ready. Good underwriting is crucial to distinguish potential borrowers who may not be ready from borrowers who, despite low wealth or low income, can still meet mortgage requirements and make their payments. We don't advocate giving everyone access to homeownership, nor do we advocate giving up on homeownership. Homeownership is right for those with sustainable employment, a demonstrated ability to meet financial obligations, and the earnings potential to meet the financial requirements of ownership.

Sadly, after the crisis, the characteristics of those seeking credit will change. In the fallout of this Great Recession, more loan applicants will have low wealth, low wages, limited benefits, greater income variability, unstable employment, and tainted credit. The aftermath of the Great Recession will impinge on some families longer than on others. The crisis, which evolved from a subprime mortgage problem to a credit crunch to a full-blown economic meltdown, has hurt most Americans. But it has disproportionally affected minority and lower income households—those with less wealth and thinner credit files. These families have lost wealth, have lost jobs, and have seen their credit histories devastated. All of these losses will affect future generations.

Unfortunately, lenders are unlikely to provide sustainable credit to those most affected unless regulation encourages them to do so. If the past indicates what will come, applicants' lower incomes, lower wealth, and lower credit scores will make lenders feel justified in either denying them credit or providing only high-cost credit. Moreover, mortgage lenders will not be the only ones to deny credit or issue it only at higher costs. Those who rely on credit scores to set prices for auto insurance, health insurance, and other financial products will do the same. People with low credit scores will find it harder to qualify for rental housing and for many jobs.

Geographic concentration may compound the problem because foreclosures are not evenly distributed. Not surprisingly, those same communities that saw a disproportionate share of subprime activity are now experiencing the highest incidence of foreclosure. Looking beyond the crisis, it is reasonable to expect that access to prime credit in these communities is likely to shrink due to weak values, tainted credit histories, and higher qualifying requirements. As prime credit options shrink, we are likely to see a widening of the gap between the haves and the have-nots with regard to homeownership. In a vicious circle, this will impede economic recovery for these communities, further justifying lenders in withholding credit. The benefits associated with owning a home, including the accumulation of wealth, will remain less available to residents in affected communities. Unless addressed and remedied, the disparities resulting from this unequal access to credit will be felt for generations. The racial gap in wealth and in the other benefits associated with homeownership will widen and become more firmly entrenched.

We recognize that lenders must be prudent when they extend credit, but we contend that careful underwriting and overly restrictive underwriting are different things. Our research shows that, historically, credit extended through community reinvestment lending is sustainable and has made available to many borrowers the benefits associated with homeownership. We know that before the crisis the Community Reinvestment Act motivated lenders to extend credit to low-income, low-wealth borrowers. Loans issued in accordance with the act's safety and soundness requirements proved sustainable, good for both borrowers and lenders.

With the declining number of banks and with fewer institutions subject to full review under the Community Reinvestment Act, the requirements of this legislation alone will not be enough. Community reinvestment lending has proved its worth and needs to be expanded. It seems reasonable to continue community reinvestment requirements as we emerge from the mortgage finance crisis, and we believe that expanding such obligations to other market participants is well justified. Community reinvestment lending serves a public purpose: it makes housing finance more broadly available and thereby helps distribute the benefits of homeownership. Those institutions considered too big to fail during the financial crisis accessed capital at lower cost than they could have otherwise done through the Troubled Asset Relief Program (TARP); in essence, those institutions benefited from significant government backing even though many of them were considered purely private. Because institutions thought too big to fail benefited from public support, it is not unreasonable to expect them to provide broad access to credit, just as the government-sponsored enterprises have been required to do.

Ultimately, to be viable, the mortgage finance system of the future must continue to develop in reaction to post-crisis realities. A regulatory backbone has to support this development. If it does not do so, the market will likely choose short-term profit over long-term stability, just as it did in the recent crisis. Only with effective regulation in place will the lending industry continue to innovate and resume its role in sustaining economic growth. Effective regulation of the provision of credit does not mean overregulation. On the contrary, regulation should simply provide consistent ground rules so that market partici- pants can do what they do best: innovate and create opportunities that lead to sustainable growth. That is better for all Americans.

We document a way to make homeownership work again for those who are ready. It is not very complicated: the likelihood of sustainable homeownership is enhanced by the use of the low down payment, thirty-year, fixed-rate mortgage, properly underwritten, serviced by parties who respond to appropriate incentives, and facilitated by a secondary market that responds to the capital needs of community reinvestment lenders.

If the crisis has a silver lining, it is the fact that when things are bro- ken they can be put back together in a different—and better—way. The crisis provides a rare chance to reform our mortgage lending sys- tem while ensuring broad access to the benefits of homeownership. History will judge us on the way we meet this opportunity.

Notes

Foreword

1. Brian K. Bucks and others, "Changes in U.S. Family Finances from 2004 to 2007: Evidence from the Survey of Consumer Finances," Federal Reserve Bulletin 95 (February 2009), table 9.1 (www.federalreserve.gov/pubs/oss/ oss2/2007/scf2007home.html).
2. Federal Reserve Board tabulations of Survey of Consumer Finances data, table 9.92 (www.federalreserve.gov/pubs/oss/oss2/92/scf92home.html).
3. Census Bureau, Current Population Survey/Housing Vacancy Survey, table 16 (www.census.gov/hhes/www/housing/hvs/historic/index.html).
4. Center for Responsible Lending, "Foreclosures by Race and Ethnicity: The Demographics of a Crisis" (Durham, N.C.: 2010).

Chapter 1

1. Rates for 2010 are the percent of all first mortgage loans in foreclosure as of the second quarter. See Mortgage Bankers Association, National Delinquency Survey (2010) (Moody's Analytics' Databuffet.com). Foreclosure rates for the Great Depression are for nonfarm real estate. See David C. Wheelock, "The Federal Response to Home Mortgage Distress: Lessons from the Great Depression," Federal Reserve Bank of St. Louis Review 90, no. 3 (2008): 133–48.
2. The exact number of banks listed as having failed since January 1, 2007, may be found on the FDIC Failed Bank List (www.fdic.gov/bank/individual/ failed/banklist.html). For loss in equity, see Federal Reserve, "B.100 Balance Sheet of Households and Nonprofit Organizations, March 11, 2010" (Washington: 2010). On the Wall Street debacle, see Johan Norberg, Financial Fiasco:

How America's Infatuation with Homeownership and Easy Money Created the Economic Crisis (Washington: Cato Institute, 2009); Joe Nocera, "Wake-up Time for a Dream," *New York Times*, June 7, 2010; Russell Roberts, "How Government Stoked the Mania," *Wall Street Journal*, October 3, 2008; and Robert Samuelson, "The Homeownership Obsession," *Newsweek*, August 4, 2008.

3. Richard K. Green and Susan M. Wachter, "The American Mortgage in Historical and International Context," *Journal of Economic Perspectives* 19, no. 4 (2005): 93–114.

4. U.S. Census Bureau, Housing and Household Economic Statistics Division, *Historical Census of Housing Tables: Homeownership* (www.census.gov/hhes/www/housing/census/historic/owner.html).

5. U.S. Census Bureau, Housing and Household Economic Statistics Division, *Housing Vacancies and Homeownership: Annual Statistics 2007* (www.census.gov/hhes/www/housing/hvs/annual07/ann07t20.html).

6. U.S. Census Bureau News, "Residential Vacancies and Homeownership in the Fourth Quarter of 2010" (www.census.gov/hhes/www/housing/hvs/qtr410/files/q410press.pdf).

7. Although they were established as government agencies, Fannie Mae and Freddie Mac were by then government-sponsored enterprises owned by stockholders. Their public-private nature meant that they remained instruments of public policy, and it also meant these two giants of the secondary market could borrow capital at a preferential rate.

8. For net wealth statistics, see Melvin L. Oliver and Thomas M. Shapiro, "Race and Wealth," *Review of Black Political Economy* 17, no. 4 (1989): 5–25.

9. Arthur B. Kennickell and Martha Starr-McCluer, "Family Finances in the U.S.: Recent Evidence from the Survey of Consumer Finances," *Federal Reserve Bulletin* 83, no. 1 (1997): 1–25.

10. We provide more detail about how CAP works—and about how well it works—in chapter 4.

11. We describe the loan rating system in chapter 3.

Chapter 2

1. Lauren Kim, "The Promotion of Homeownership as an Overriding Goal," *Wall Street Journal*, March 19, 2008 (http://blogs.wsj.com/developments/2008/03/19/the-promotion-of-homeownership-as-an-overriding-goal).

2. Eric Toder and others, "Reforming the Mortgage Interest Deduction" (Washington: Urban Institute, 2010) (www.urban.org/UploadedPDF/412099-mortgage-deduction-reform.pdf).

3. For instance, the average value of the mortgage interest payment deduction rises with income, from $91 for those with annual incomes less than $40,000 to $5,459 for those making more than $250,000. See James Poterba and Todd Sinai, "Tax Expenditures for Owner-Occupied Housing: Deductions for Property Taxes and Mortgage Interest and the Exclusion of Imputed Rental Income," *American Economic Review* 98, no. 2 (2008): 84–89.

4. Zhu Xiao Di, *Housing Wealth and Household Net Wealth in the United States: A New Profile Based on the Recently Released 2001 SCF Data* (Cambridge, Mass.: Joint Center for Housing Studies, 2003).

5. William M. Rohe and Leslie S. Stewart, "Homeownership and Neighborhood Stability," *Housing Policy Debate* 7, no. 1 (1996): 37–81; Chris Hamnett, "The Relationship between Residential Migration and Housing Tenure in London, 1971–81," *Environment and Planning* 23 (1991): 1147–62; Scott J. South and Glenn D. Deane, "Race and Residential Mobility: Individual Determinants and Structural Constraints," *Social Forces* 72, no. 1 (1993): 147–67.

6. John I. Gilderbloom and John P. Markham, "The Impact of Homeownership on Political Beliefs," *Social Forces* 73, no. 4 (1995): 1589–607; Denise DiPasquale and Edward L. Glaeser, "Incentives and Social Capital: Are Homeowners Better Citizens?" *Journal of Urban Economics* 45, no. 2 (1999): 354–84; William M. Rohe and Michael A. Stegman, "The Impact of Home Ownership on the Social and Political Involvement of Low-Income People," *Urban Affairs Review* 30, no. 1 (1994): 152–72; Kim Manturuk, Mark Lindblad, and Roberto Quercia, "Homeownership and Local Voting in Disadvantaged Urban Neighborhoods," *Cityscape* 11 (2009): 105–22.

7. Kim Manturuk, Mark Lindblad, and Roberto G. Quercia, "Friends and Neighbors: Homeownership and Social Capital among Low- to Moderate-Income Families," *Journal of Urban Affairs* 32, no. 4 (2010): 471–88.

8. Richard K. Green and Susan M. Wachter, "The American Mortgage in Historical and International Context," *Journal of Economic Perspectives* 19, no. 4 (2005): 93–114.

9. "Making Sense of the Fannie and Freddie Problems," *New York Times*, July 11, 2008 (www.nytimes.com/interactive/2008/07/11/business/20080711_fannie_graphic.html).

10. In 1981 Fannie Mae issued its first mortgage pass-through and called it a mortgage-backed security. Freddie Mac had issued its first mortgage pass-through (called a participation certificate) a decade earlier. Ginnie Mae had guaranteed the first mortgage pass-through security of an approved lender in 1968.

11. Unlike the current crisis, the S&L crisis was triggered by a rate mismatch—that is, by the fact that the S&Ls were paying higher interest on deposits than they were charging on the long-term mortgages they'd made. However,

reckless lending due to deregulation and poor oversight played a central role in that and the current financial crises.

12. Gregory D. Squires, "Community Reinvestment: An Emerging Social Movement," in *From Redlining to Reinvestment: Community Responses to Urban Disinvestment,* edited by Gregory D. Squires (Temple University Press, 1992), pp. 1–37.

13. Calvin Bradford, "Financing Home Ownership: The Federal Role in Neighborhood Decline," *Urban Affairs Quarterly* 14, no. 3 (1979): 313–35.

14. Quoted in Squires, "Community Reinvestment," p. 5.

15. Ibid., p. 4.

16. Bradford, "Financing Home Ownership," p. 323.

17. "About Ginnie Mae," 2010 (www.ginniemae.gov/about/about.asp?sub Title=About).

18. Kevin R. Kosar, "Government Sponsored Enterprises (GSEs): An Institutional Overview," Report (Washington: Congressional Research Service, 2008).

19. Davie J. Reiss, "The Federal Government's Implied Guarantee of Fannie Mae and Freddie Mac's Obligations: Uncle Sam Will Pick up the Tab," *Georgia Law Review* 42 (2008): 1019–81.

20. Julie Creswell, "Protected by Washington, Companies Boomed," *New York Times,* July 13, 2008.

21. Alicia H. Munnell and others, "Mortgage Lending in Boston: Interpreting HMDA Data," *American Economic Review* 86, no. 1 (1992): 25–53.

22. Roberto G. Quercia, George W. McCarthy, and Susan M. Wachter, "The Impacts of Affordable Lending Efforts on Homeownership Rates," *Journal of Housing Economics* 12, no. 1 (2003): 29–59; Paul S. Calem and Susan M. Wachter, "Community Reinvestment and Credit Risk: Evidence from an Affordable Home Loan Program," *Real Estate Economics* 27, no. 1 (1999): 105–34.

23. Christopher Herbert, "Re-examining Efforts to Promote Homeownership: What Have We Learned from the Foreclosure Crisis?" Paper prepared for conference, Challenges and Opportunities for Homeownership in a New Banking Era, May 6, 2009.

24. Harold L. Bunce and Randall M. Scheessele, "The GSE's Funding of Affordable Loans," Working Paper HF-001 (Washington: Office of Policy Development and Research, U.S. Department of Housing and Urban Development, 1996).

25. This assumes that each mortgage would have been for $79,000, the median amount for the CAP portfolio.

26. Except for figures concerning marriage/partnership, presence of children, and education, all figures are taken from the "Self-Help CAP Portfolio Report," June 11, 2010.

Chapter 3

1. Paul McCulley, "The Shadow Banking System and Hyman Minsky's Economic Journey," 2009 (http://europe.pimco.com/LeftNav/Featured+Mar ket+Commentary/FF/2009/Global+Central+Bank+Focus+May+2009+Shadow+ Banking+and+Minsky+McCulley.htm).

2. Garn–St. Germain Depository Institutions Act of 1982, Title VIII, Alternative Mortgage Transactions, *FDIC Law, Regulations, Related Acts* (www.fdic.gov/regulations/laws/rules/8000-4100.html).

3. Souphala Chomsisengphet and Anthony Pennington-Cross, "The Evolution of the Subprime Mortgage Market," *Federal Reserve Bank of St. Louis Review* 88, no. 1 (2006): 31–56.

4. Inside Mortgage Finance, *The 2008 Mortgage Market Statistical Annual* (Bethesda, Md.: 2008).

5. The Associates started in 1918 as an independent finance company and boasts that it was the first finance company to offer credit life insurance (in 1951). In 1968 it was purchased by Gulf+Western (later known as Paramount Communications); it was sold to Ford Motor Company in 1989, Ford's largest acquisition to that point. In 1996 Ford took the company public. In 2000 the company was acquired by Citigroup, and its consumer lending business was folded into CitiFinancial. Though the merger generated protests from community advocates, it made Citigroup the number one B- and C-grade lender of 2000 (www.citi.com/citi/corporate/history/associates.htm).

6. Timothy Geithner, "Credit Market Innovations and Their Implications," speech delivered at the 2007 Credit Markets Symposium hosted by the Federal Reserve Bank of Richmond in Charlotte, N.C. (www.newyorkfed.org/news events/speeches/2007/gei070323.html).

7. Alan Greenspan, "Remarks by Chairman Alan Greenspan: Consumer Finance," delivered at the Federal Reserve System's Fourth Annual Community Affairs Research Conference, Washington, D.C., April 8, 2005 (www.federal reserve.gov/boarddocs/speeches/2005/20050408/default.htm).

8. Inside Mortgage Finance, *The 2010 Mortgage Market Statistical Annual* (Bethesda, Md.: 2010).

9. Robert M. Hunt, "The Development and Regulation of Consumer Credit Reporting in America," Working Paper 02-21 (Philadelphia: Federal Reserve Bank of Philadelphia, 2002).

10. Board of Governors of the Federal Reserve System, "Report to the Congress on Credit Scoring and Its Effects on the Availability and Affordability of Credit" (Washington: August 2007); Jonathan Spader, "Beyond Disparate Impact: Risk-Based Pricing and Disparity in Consumer Credit History Scores," Working Paper (Center for Community Capital, University of North Carolina, 2009).

11. John Straka, "A Shift in the Mortgage Landscape: The 1990s Move to Automated Credit Evaluations," *Journal of Housing Research* 11, no. 2 (2000): 207–32; Robert B. Avery and others, "Credit Scoring: Statistical Issues and Evidence from Credit-Bureau Files," *Real Estate Economics* 28, no. 3 (2000): 523–47.

12. Greenspan, "Remarks."

13. Greg Ip and Mark Whitehouse, "Huge Flood of Capital to Invest Spurs World-Wide Risk Taking," *Wall Street Journal*, November 3, 2005.

14. This section and subsequent passages in this chapter are drawn from Roberto G. Quercia, "Exposing the Myth of Irrational Exuberance," *Huffington Post*, September 8, 2009 (www.huffingtonpost.com/roberto-g-querica/exposing-the-myth-of-irra_b_279682.html).

15. U.S. Securities and Exchange Commission, "Roundtable to Examine Oversight of Credit Rating Agencies," Briefing paper, 2009 (www.sec.gov/spot light/cra-oversight-roundtable/briefing-paper.htm).

16. Gretchen Morgenson, "Arcane Market Is Next to Face Big Credit Test," *New York Times*, February 17, 2008.

17. Alan Greenspan, "Understanding Household Debt Obligations," remarks delivered at the Credit Union National Association Governmental Affairs Conference, Washington, D.C., February 23, 2004 (www.federal reserve.gov/boarddocs/speeches/2004/20040223/).

18. Axel A. Weber, "Moral Hazard, Market Discipline, and Self-Regulation: What Have We Learnt?" speech delivered at the Fiftieth Anniversary of Bank Negara Malaysia, February 10, 2009.

19. Paul E. Gabriel, "A Longitudinal Examination of Earnings Inequality and Mobility among Young, Full-Time Workers in the United States," *Social Science Journal* 42 (2005): 603–03.

20. Chomsisengphet and Pennington-Cross, "The Evolution of the Subprime Mortgage Market."

21. Center for Responsive Politics, "Influence and Lobbying: Interest Groups, Summary," 2010 (www.opensecrets.org/industries/indus.php?ind=f).

22. Lei Ding and others, "The Neighborhood Patterns of Higher-Priced Lending: The Case of Atlanta," *Journal of Affordable Housing and Community Development Law* 17, no. 3 (2008): 193–217.

23. Robert Van Order and Peter Zorn, "Income, Location, and Default: Some Implications for Community Lending," *Real Estate Economics* 28, no. 3 (2000): 385–404; Robert F. Cotterman, *Neighborhood Effects in Mortgage Default Risk* (Washington: Office of Policy Development and Research, U.S. Department of Housing and Urban Development, 2001).

24. Lei Ding, Roberto G. Quercia, and Janneke Ratcliffe, "The Spillover Effect of Neighborhood Subprime Lending," paper prepared for the AREUEA meeting, Washington, 2008.

25. William P. Alexander and others, "Some Loans Are More Equal than Others: Third–Party Originations and Defaults in the Subprime Mortgage Industry," *Real Estate Economics* 30, no. 4 (2002): 667–97.

26. A study by First American LoanPerformance on behalf of the *Wall Street Journal* found that more than half of subprime loans went to borrowers with credit scores over 620, including a third of borrowers with credit scores over 660. See Rick Brooks and Ruth Simon, "Subprime Debacle Traps Even Very Credit-Worthy," *Wall Street Journal*, December 3, 2007 (http://online.wsj.com/article/SB119662974358911035.html).

27. Marsha J. Courchane, Brian J. Surette, and Peter M. Zorn, "Subprime Borrowers: Mortgage Transitions and Outcomes," *Journal of Real Estate Finance and Economics* 24, no. 4 (2004): 365–92.

Chapter 4

1. Federal Reserve Bank of Dallas, "The CRA and Subprime Lending: Discerning the Difference," *Banking and Community Perspectives*, issue 1 (2009) (www.dallasfed.org/ca/bcp/2009/bcp0901.cfm).

2. Jonathan S. Spader and Roberto G. Quercia, "Community Reinvestment Lending in a Changing Context: Evidence of Interaction with FHA and Subprime Originations," Working Paper (Center for Community Capital, University of North Carolina, 2009).

3. Lei Ding and others, "Risky Borrowers or Risky Mortgages: Disaggregating Effects Using Propensity Score Models," Working Paper (Center for Community Capital, University of North Carolina, 2008).

4. Harold L. Bunce and others, *Subprime Foreclosures: The Smoking Gun of Predatory Lending?* (U.S. Department of Housing and Urban Development, 2001).

5. Edward M. Gramlich, "Remarks by Governor Edward M. Gramlich at the Federal Reserve Bank of Philadelphia Community and Consumer Affairs Department Conference on Predatory Lending," December 6, 2000.

6. Roberto G. Quercia, Michael A. Stegman, and Walter R. Davis, "The Impact of Predatory Loan Terms on Subprime Foreclosures: The Special Case of Prepayment Penalties and Balloon Payments," Working Paper (Center for Community Capital, University of North Carolina, 2005).

7. Rates of serious delinquency come from Mortgage Bankers Association, *National Delinquency Survey* (2009) (Moody's Analytics' Databuffet.com). Figures are from the fourth quarter of 2009.

8. Amaad Rivera and others, "Foreclosed: State of the Dream 2008" (Boston: United for a Fair Economy, 2008).

9. Dean Baker, codirector of the Center for Economic and Policy Research, testimony before the House Financial Institutions Subcommittee of the Finan-

cial Services Committee, March 4, 2009 (www.cepr.net/index.php/publica tions/testimony/tarp-broader-economy).

10. Federal Reserve, "B.100 Balance Sheet of Households and Nonprofit Organizations, March 11, 2010" (Washington: 2010).

11. Tracy Turner, "Does Investment Risk Affect the Housing Decisions of Families?" *Economic Inquiry* 41, no. 4 (2003): 675–92; Christian A. L. Hilber, "Neighborhood Externality Risk and the Homeownership Status of Properties," *Journal of Urban Economics* 57, no. 2 (2005): 213–41.

12. Vladimir Klyuev and Paul Mills, "Is Housing Wealth an 'ATM'? The Relationship between Household Wealth, Home Equity Withdrawal, and Saving Rates," *IMF Staff Papers* 54, no. 3 (2007): 539–62; John D. Benjamin and Peter Chinloy, "Home Equity, Household Savings, and Consumption," *Journal of Real Estate Finance and Economics* 37, no. 1 (2008): 21–33.

13. Allison Freeman and Bruce Desmarais, "Portfolio Adjustment to Home Equity Accumulation among CRA Borrowers," Working Paper (Center for Community Capital, University of North Carolina, 2010).

14. Amy Crews Cutts and Richard K. Green, "Innovative Servicing Technology: Smart Enough to Keep People in Their Houses?" Working Paper 04-03 (Washington: Freddie Mac, 2004) (www.inevitablechange.org/studies/innova tive_Servicing_ technology.pdf).

15. Ibid.

16. Michael A. Stegman and others, "Preventive Servicing Is Good for Business and Affordable Homeownership Policy," *Housing Policy Debate* 18, no. 2 (2007): 243–78.

17. Center for Responsible Lending, "A Snapshot of the Subprime Market," 2007 (www.responsiblelending.org/mortgage-lending/tools-resources/snapshot-of-the-subprime-market.pdf).

18. Jonathan S. Spader and Roberto G. Quercia, "Mobility and Exit from Homeownership: Implications for CRA Lending," *Housing Policy Debate* 19, no. 4 (2008): 675–709.

19. Among ARM borrowers, this rate of refinance reflects the current interest rate of the mortgage at the time of the interview. Because only 19 percent of the refinanced ARMs had reset from the introductory rate at that time, the refinanced rate primarily reflects the introductory rate received by ARM borrowers.

20. Jonathan S. Spader and Roberto G. Quercia, "The Refinancing Transition: Equity Extraction, Income Constraints, and Subprime Refinancing among CRA Mortgage Borrowers," Working Paper (Center for Community Capital, University of North Carolina, 2009).

Chapter 5

1. Mortgage Bankers Association, *National Delinquency Survey* (2009) (Moody's Analytics' Databuffet.com).

2. Ibid. Figures are for the fourth quarter of 2009.

3. U.S. Government Accountability Office, *Loan Performance and Negative Home Equity in the Nonprime Mortgage Market* (2009) (www.gao.gov/new.items/d10146r.pdf).

4. Only 3.5 percent of respondents became unmarried or separated during this period, so it is unlikely that changes in family structure played a large role in the financial difficulties of most of these households.

5. Some will wonder how approximately 17 percent of these 315 owners could blame unemployment for their delayed housing payments when only 6 percent of owners or their spouses became unemployed between 2008 and 2009. Because of how survey questions were worded, those who identified unemployment as a cause of their delayed housing payment might have been referring to job loss that had occurred before 2008, or they might have been referring to the loss of one of several jobs held.

6. This section draws from Kimberly Manturuk, Sarah Riley, and Janneke Ratcliffe. "Perception and Reality during the Financial Crisis: Homeownership, Low-Income Households, and Financial Stress," Paper prepared for the First Annual Boulder Summer Conference on Consumer Financial Decision Making, Boulder, Colo., summer 2010.

7. Mark Lindblad and others, "Coping with Adversity: Personal Bankruptcy among Lower Income Homeowners," Working Paper (Center for Community Capital, University of North Carolina, 2011).

8. Our six-item scale measures how much stress people experience as a result of financial difficulties. Respondents were asked how stressful they find each of the following four situations: paying their rent or mortgage, maintaining their dwelling, managing their money, and saving for retirement. Responses are coded 0 for not at all stressful, 1 for somewhat stressful, and 2 for very stressful. Respondents were also asked to rate two questions as not at all true (0), somewhat true (1), or very true (2). The questions are, How true is it that you pay too much rent or mortgage? and How true is it that you have too much debt? The six responses are summed to create an index of financial stress.

9. We measure overall stress using the four-item perceived stress scale (PSS) of Sheldon Cohen, Tom Kamarck, and Robin Mermelstein, "A Global Measure of Perceived Stress," *Journal of Health and Social Behavior* 24, no. 4 (1983): 385–96. The PSS measures the degree to which respondents found their lives unpredictable, uncontrollable, and overloading. See also Sheldon Cohen and Gail M. Williamson, "Perceived Stress in a Probability Sample of the United States," in *The Social Psychology of Health: Claremont Symposium on Applied*

Social Psychology, edited by Shirlynn Spacapan and Stuart Oskamp (Newbury Park, Calif.: Sage, 1988). The PSS consists of the following four questions: In the last month, how often have you felt that you were unable to control the important things in your life? In the last month, how often have you felt confident about your ability to handle your personal problems? In the last month, how often have you felt that things were going your way? In the last month, how often have you felt difficulties were piling up so high that you could not overcome them? Each of the four items has the following response options: never (0), almost never (1), sometimes (2), fairly often (3), and very often (4). Two of the items are reverse coded, and then the four items are summed to create the stress score. Scores range from 0 (no stress) to 16 (high stress). The scale is descriptive rather than diagnostic.

10. We measure financial satisfaction using a single question, How satisfied are you with your overall financial situation? The three response options are very satisfied, somewhat satisfied, and not at all satisfied.

Chapter 6

1. Allen Krinsman, "Subprime Mortgage Meltdown: How Did It Happen and How Will It End?" *Journal of Structured Finance* 13, no. 2 (2007): 13–19.

2. Amy Crews Cutts and Richard K. Green, 2004, "Innovative Servicing Technology: Smart Enough to Keep People in Their Houses?" Working Paper 04-03 (Washington: Freddie Mac) (www.inevitablechange.org/studies/innova tive_Servicing_technology.pdf).

Chapter 7

1. Dodd-Frank Wall Street Reform and Consumer Protection Act, H. Rept. 4173, 111 Cong. 2 sess. (Government Printing Office, 2010).

2. We relied upon the following sources for this overview: ibid.; Stacy Kaper, "Now for the Hard Part: Writing All the Rules," *American Banker,* July 21, 2010; *New York Times,* "Times Topics: Financial Regulatory Reform" (http://topics.nytimes.com/topics/reference/timestopics/subjects/c/credit_crisis/ financial_regulatory_reform/index.html?inline=nyt-classifier); Brief Summary of the Dodd-Frank Wall Street Reform and Consumer Protection Act, Senate Banking, Housing, and Urban Affairs Committee (http://banking.senate.gov/ public/_files/070110_Dodd_Frank_Wall_Street_Reform_comprehensive_summ ary_Final.pdf).

3. See http://banking.senate.gov/Brief Summary of the Dodd-Frank Wall Street Reform and Consumer Protection Act. Subsequent references to the act refer to this summary.

4. In addition, the law bans the inclusion of single-premium credit insurance at mortgage origination; promotes strong assignee liability, which is expected to lead to originators holding in portfolio those loans that trigger HOEPA requirements; and mandates the licensing of originators, imposing upon them a duty of care.

Chapter 8

1. Ben Bernanke, "Regulation and Financial Innovation," speech delivered at the Federal Reserve Bank of Atlanta's 2007 Financial Markets Conference, Sea Island, Georgia (www.federalreserve.gov/newsevents/speech/bernanke 20070515a.htm).

2. Susan Hoffman, *Politics and Banking* (Johns Hopkins University Press, 2001), p. 5.

3. Bernanke, "Regulation and Financial Innovation."

4. Ibid.

5. Dan Immergluck, *Foreclosed: High-Risk Lending, Deregulation, and the Undermining of America's Mortgage Market* (Cornell University Press, 2009), p. 222.

6. Jennifer Harmon, "BB&T Starts 10% Haircut for Quality," *National Mortgage News* 34, no. 31 (2010): 1–10.

7. Paul Muolo, "Buyers May Ask Sellers for Reserves," *National Mortgage News* 34, no. 32 (2010): 1–10.

8. New capital and leverage requirements are being determined in accordance with the Dodd-Frank Act.

9. U.S. Department of Housing and Urban Development's Office of Policy Development and Research, "Report to Congress on the Root Causes of the Foreclosure Crisis," 2010 (www.huduser.org/Publications/PDF/Foreclosure_09.pdf).

Index

150   *Index*

2408516

CPSIA information can be obtained at www.ICGtesting.com
Printed in the USA
LVOW040503020213

318284LV00001B/147/P